A Catholic Primer
on the Ecumenical Movement

Woodstock Papers

Occasional Essays for Theology

PREPARED BY

Professors of the Faculty of Theology
Woodstock College, Woodstock, Maryland

EDITED BY

JOHN COURTNEY MURRAY, S.J.
WALTER J. BURGHARDT, S.J.

No. 1

THE NEWMAN PRESS

WESTMINSTER, MARYLAND
1957

A Catholic Primer

on the

Ecumenical Movement

by GUSTAVE WEIGEL, S.J.
Professor of Ecclesiology
Woodstock College

THE NEWMAN PRESS

WESTMINSTER, MARYLAND

1957

The present study is a partially revised version of an article which appeared under the same name in *The Thomist Reader: 1957* (Baltimore: Thomist Press, 1957) pp. 18–70.

Imprimi Potest: WILLIAM F. MALONEY, S.J.
Præp. Prov. Marylandiæ

Nihil Obstat: EDWARD A. CERNY, S.S., D.D.
Censor Librorum

Imprimatur: ✠ FRANCIS P. KEOUGH, D.D.
Archbishop of Baltimore

October 29, 1957

⋆ General Preface ⋆

THEOLOGY is today a matter of interest to a public far more extensive and varied than the audience housed within the walls of seminaries and schools of divinity. This is not a reference to that type of popularization which almost of necessity involves the sacrifice of theological accuracy. There is question here rather of that widespread interest on the part of the non-specialist which demands that theology be presented in terms intelligible to him. At the same time that he satisfies this demand, the theologian hopes that his contribution will be of interest and assistance to his colleagues in the field.

Like their colleagues in the other Catholic seminaries of the United States, the Jesuit professors who constitute the Pontifical Faculty of Theology at Woodstock, Maryland, have tried to satisfy this interest by their books and public lectures. But theirs is a growing conviction that there is room for a medium through which their reflections can be communicated, a medium other than the technical theological journals, less substantial than a book, less superficial than a lecture.

Another periodical hardly seems to be the answer. The professors of Woodstock College think rather in terms of a series of studies, occasional papers, in which their meditations on theological questions and on themes which can be illumined by theology may be presented. The WOODSTOCK PAPERS have been projected to meet this need. Several brochures in the series will appear each year. They will have a wide variety of subjects, but each will have some relevance to theology. The papers will be scholarly, but not for the specialist. It is hoped that they will be not unworthy of the theologian's notice, yet of interest and profit to those who are not theologians.

The WOODSTOCK PAPERS will be the voice of the Woodstock Faculty of Theology, but by way of exception the series will include contributions by authors who are not members of the Woodstock Faculty. The brochures in the series will vary in length and will include, when a wider public interest seems to call for them, reprints from more specialized media.

The editorial offices of the quarterly, THEOLOGICAL STUDIES, are located at Woodstock College. The editorial staff of that periodical will act also as editorial staff of the WOODSTOCK PAPERS: John Courtney Murray, S.J., and Walter J. Burghardt, S.J., as Editors, Edmond F. X. Ivers, S.J., as Business Manager.

The professors of Woodstock College are grateful to Mr. J. William Eckenrode, of the Newman Press, who has graciously agreed to publish the new venture.

JOSEPH F. MURPHY, S.J.

Rector, Woodstock College (1951–1957)

★ Contents ★

★ Introduction ★

MANY A HIGHLY significant phenomenon is not always understood by the generation which is present to it. It is very easy for Catholics, even theologians, to be very hazy concerning what is undoubtedly the most striking ecclesiological event since the sixteenth-century Reformation. The older generation of Catholic theology professors in America did not feel it urgent to keep in touch with the movements fermenting in the Christianity beyond the Church, and something of their innocent unawareness still darkens the halls of our theology centers. In consequence, the frequent references to the ecumenical movement in our journals of current events and current thought leave many of our Catholic thinkers, theological and non-theological, in an uncomfortable mist. They feel that something important is going on but they are quite uninformed about the facts and their relevance.

The purpose of the present unpretentious study is to convey elementary data concerning the ecumenical movement for the benefit of Catholics interested in theological matters. Advisedly, the report is called a primer; for it wishes to supply only basic information concerning that concatenation of facts, moods, and hopes which is today labeled as the ecumenical movement.[1] The primer is for Catholics, and so not only non-Catholic ecumenism[2] is considered but its Catholic counterpart as well. Since the little treatise is composed with a theological dynamism, a theological meditation will be added to the facts.

We shall begin from the moment in which we are. First, we shall see non-Catholic ecumenism as palpably expressed by the World Council of Churches. After describing its structure, we shall take a glimpse of its immediate past, and conclude with a timid gaze at its immediate future without the aid of a crystal ball. Secondly, we shall consider the different manifestations of Catholic ecumenism. The third part of the study will be a confrontation of Catholic theology with ecumenism.

A Catholic Primer
on the Ecumenical Movement

★ 1 ★

Non-Catholic Ecumenism:
The World Council of Churches

I. THE PRESENT

(a) *Essence*

In the late summer of 1948, from August 22 to September 4, a period of two weeks, there was held at Amsterdam in Holland the first Assembly of the World Council of Churches.[3] 147 churches from 44 countries were represented by 351 delegates and 238 alternates. The invitations to the meeting were extended by a committee acting as an entity called "The World Council of Churches—In Process of Formation." The Assembly itself established the World Council of Churches by framing a brief constitution. Because of this constitution adopted by the Amsterdam Assembly on August 30, 1948, and slightly amended at the second Assembly at Evanston, Illinois, 1956, plus the body of rules also amended by the Evanston Assembly on August 26, 1954, we can speak accurately and objectively concerning the organization.[4]

In the light of the constitution and rules we can say:

1. The Council "is a fellowship of Churches which accept our Lord Jesus Christ as God and Saviour."

2. There is no other definition of the Council given by the constitution than the one cited. However, the constitu-

[3]

tion indicates the powers and functions of the Council, which implicitly help to define the nature of the union.

3. In the fourth article of the constitution, under the heading "Authority," we find the powers which the member churches of the Council gave to it. By considering these powers we can understand better the nature of the fellowship affirmed in the definition. There is nowhere in the constitution a definition of the words: "churches," "accept," "God," or "Saviour."

4. In the fourth article the constitution declares that the Council "shall offer counsel and provide opportunity of united action in matters of common interest." This is the first power of the Council. Its secondary powers are: (*a*) "to take action on behalf of constituent Churches in such matters as one or more of them may commit to it"; (*b*) "to call regional and world conferences on specific subjects as occasion may require." The powers of the Council are severely restricted. "The World Council shall not legislate for the Churches; nor shall it act for them in any manner except as indicated above or as may hereafter be specified by the constituent Churches."

5. Hence it follows that the Council is neither a church nor the Church. The Council cannot define doctrine, polity, or interdenominational policy. No member church is obliged by any doctrinal or practical recommendation of the Council, nor can the Council do more than present to the churches the fruits of the discussions held under Council auspices. What the member churches wish to do with such expressions is left entirely to the discretion of the churches themselves.

It is important to recognize the very limited authority of the Council. It can make no laws for the churches; it can impose no doctrine; it cannot even have or define a doctrine of its own. It wishes only to provide opportunity for discussion and common contribution to the solution of questions. It also formulates and distributes the findings of such conversations. However, the literature of the spokesmen for the Council abounds with the faith that the Holy Spirit will guide the debates so that what does come forth will bear the authority of truth which cannot help but move the churches. However, one and all make it anxiously clear that there will be no legal, parliamentary, or juridical coercion of the churches, which retain their completely unimpaired freedom in their own communities.

Yet all is not said by the jejune phrases of the constitution. We must distinguish between the scope of the Council and its hope. Beyond the very limited scope of union as expressly and pithily stated by the constitution, there is present in all participants a strong ecumenical hope which goes far ahead of the constitutional declarations. The hope will always be cautiously phrased lest anyone see in its concrete expressions a threat of regimentation. The hope is, of course, that all the separations, dogmatic and structural, which divide the churches disappear altogether. The goal is a united Christian Church.

In this ecumenical hope of ultimate union one notes profound divergences. The Byzantine Oriental members of the Council consistently make it clear that the one true and visible Church of Christ already exists and it is the Eastern Byzantine communion, into which all the others must enter, though proper consideration for local and historical eccentricities will be made. The Anglo-Catholics go along with the Byzantines, except that they would insist that the one Church of Christ is the Holy Catholic Church, which is not

[5]

to be identified with the Byzantine Church exclusively, since it includes the Old Catholic groups and the Anglican communion.

In complete opposition to such views we find some activist evangelicals who consider the Church as an inner bond of the Spirit manifested in individual faith, so that the external organization flowering from the collective faith of congregations is not to be determined a priori but is optional according to the wishes of the gathered faithful. Nor are the evangelicals all of one mind. Some of them are liberal, persuaded that the structure and dogmas of the Church are the free creations of the believing communities. De facto you always have them, but de jure you do not need them. Faith, which is a personal, experiential achievement, is all that is required. Other evangelicals are closer to the Reform tradition, and give importance in varying degrees to the Scriptures as obligatory norms for order and belief, but no other obligations can be imposed. These latter would demand some scriptural formula of unity of doctrine and practice. Let it be added here that at the moment the Byzantine Orientals and Anglo-Catholics represent a relatively small minority to which the Old Catholics add their slight weight.

Fundamentalists who insist on sharply defined traditional scriptural formulas of belief keep away from the Council and will have no part in it, because they find that the Council is not committed to a high degree of biblical literalism, which fundamentalists consider essential to valid Christianity.

In the light of these facts we must distinguish the unity achieved by the Council as organized by the constitution from the future unity ardently hoped for by the participants in Council activities. This hope is not alien or incidental to the unity of the fellowship. In article 3 of the constitution one of the functions enumerated as proper to the Council is "to promote the growth of ecumenical consciousness in the members of all Churches." However, the Council juridically as such does not represent a church-union but rather an opportunity for the disunited churches to meet in an atmosphere of harmony and friendship. Strictly speaking, it is not an ecumenical fusion but only a possible means to that end. As it is constituted, the Council is not the Church, is not a confederated church, is not an amalgamated church, is not the initiation of a fusion of churches. It is a gathering locus for distinct, separate, autonomous churches, with the fervent hope that in such a locus under the guidance of grace the churches meeting will to an ever greater degree unite among themselves in terms of their own individual initiative. The World Council is like the evangelical conception of a sacrament. It does not produce a given grace, but it is the stimulating occasion in which the churches can elicit acts under grace given immediately by God.

(b) *Membership*

According to article 2 of the constitution, churches are eligible to admission into the Council if they "express their agreement with the basis [i.e., the definition as cited above] upon which the Council is founded." In addition there is required a conformity with "the criteria as the Assembly or the Central Committee may prescribe." The criteria are declared in the rules. The first rule describes the conditions required for membership, and section 1 of the rule tells us that either autonomous churches or denominational unions of autonomous churches can be accepted as members. Section 3 of the rule expressly indicates four considerations which should guide the Council in admitting churches as members. The church in question must be autonomous, even though it belongs to a denominational union, or to a common confession. As far as the rule makes it clear, autonomy means that the church is not responsible to any other church for its life and conduct. The church must also be stable, which means that it shows cohesion and stability in terms of historical perdurance with a solid promise of continued survival. Its size also must be taken into consideration, but no concrete norms are given for this task. If the applicant church passes these tests, and others which the Council can make at its discretion, it will be admitted, provided that no more than a third of the member churches oppose its admission.

There are many ambiguities in these regulations. The basic law is that the churches "accept our Lord Jesus Christ as God and Saviour." Yet this law is reworded in two different forms in the rules. Rule I, 3 understands the word "accept" as "express agreement with the Basis upon which the Council is formed." Rule XI, 2, g, (i) widens the understanding to this degree: "accept the Basis of the World Council of Churches or express its willingness to co-operate on that Basis."

Hence, the Unitarian churches are not antecedently excluded from membership in the Council just because they do not believe in the divinity of Christ. They can join as long as they are willing to cooperate on the basis of Christ's divinity, no matter what they believe themselves.

Likewise, there are many theologians of member churches who do not believe in the divinity of Christ in the Nicene sense. The constitution has no intention of incommoding them. It does not define what it means by divinity, nor does it suppose the Nicene interpretation. Hence, an Arian understanding of Christ's divinity, or some accommodated understanding whereby divinity can be meaningfully applied to a mere human being, is acceptable as far as the Council's constitution demands. We must always remember that the Council neither presupposes nor prescribes unity in belief. Consequently, in the light of the constitution, Unitarians, Witnesses of Jehovah, Nestorians, and (if there are any) Arians are conceivably eligible for membership.

The word "church" is also ambiguous; for there is no definition of it anywhere. For 1955 the Council gives the number of churches which are members as 164, representing 46 countries and over 160,000,000 believers.[5] One of the British members of the Council is the Salvation Army. But in the minds of some observers the Salvation Army is not so much a church as a non-denominational evangelical group engaged in witness and charity. Likewise, in the Official Report of the Amsterdam Assembly, Germany has four membership units in the Council.[6] In the Evanston Report this still holds, but one of the membership units is broken down.[7] The unit itself is the Evangelical Church in Germany, which is made up of twenty-seven regional churches, divided into three groups: Lutheran, Reformed, and United. After Amsterdam, the General Synod of the United Lutheran Churches of Germany recommended that the Lutheran churches within the Evangelical Union declare themselves members *proprio jure* of the World Council— which ten of them did. Hence, they go as delegates of the Lutheran churches but also represent the Council of the

A CATHOLIC PRIMER ON

Evangelical Church of Germany. One cannot help but ask: Which is the church—the Evangelical Church in Germany, the United Lutheran Church of Germany, or the individual regional church? The Council recognizes both the regional church and the Evangelical Church in Germany to which the regional church belongs, but in its final count of members of its Council it counts only the Evangelical Church union.

Similarly, the Anglican community of churches has not one but many units in the Council: Australia and Tasmania, Canada, Japan, New Zealand, South Africa, England, Ireland, Scotland, Wales, the Protestant Episcopal Church of America, India, West Africa, and the West Indies. Consequently, the Anglican Church has many blocs of votes in the Assembly. The Lutherans enjoy a parallel situation. Without counting the many Lutheran churches of Germany and the Continent, from the United States alone there are five Lutheran churches with membership in the Council.

The Byzantine Orientals also have multiple representation. The individual members include the Patriarchate of Alexandria, the Church of Cyprus, the Church of Greece, the Patriarchate of Jerusalem, the Patriarchate of Antioch, the Ecumenical Patriarchate of Constantinople, the Romanian Orthodox episcopate in America, the Russian Orthodox Greek Catholic Church in North America, the Syrian Antiochian Orthodox Church: Archdiocese of New York and All North America.

In the light of these facts an academic point could be raised. If the Catholic Church were to enter the Council, would she be one church and thus reduced to the level of the moribund Holy Apostolic Catholic Church of the East (Assyrian)? Or would she be divided up into units of different rites giving her some ten blocs of delegates? Or, perhaps, should she be broken up into national churches, so that there would be some sixty or seventy Catholic membership units?

The churches not in the Council must also be considered in order to measure the ecumenicity of the Council itself. The most glaring lacuna is produced by the absence of the Catholic Church, whose faithful outnumber by one hundred million the combined memberships of all the other separate Christian bodies. The Byzantine Oriental Church has its impressive numerical mass behind the Iron Curtain, but not one church of that area has as yet entered into the Council. On the other hand, no major Protestant denomination is missing, though some important churches of such denominations have not yet joined. Among the American Protestant absentees we note the influential Lutheran Church—Missouri Synod, which includes more than a third of all American Lutherans. Three American Baptist churches belong to the Council: the National Baptist Convention, Inc. (colored), comprising some 5,000,000 members; the American Baptist Convention, whose members amount to a million and a half; the Seventh Day Baptists, who number less than 7,000 members. But most of the American Baptist Churches, including the Southern Baptist Convention with more than 8,000,000 members, are missing from the Council.[8] The Unitarians, Universalists, Mormons, Pentecostals, Adventists, Witnesses of Jehovah (who refuse to call themselves a church), and Christian Scientists have not yet entered into the Council.

This rapid glance at the members of and absentees from the Council shows up the following situation. All the Oriental churches, the Armenian Gregorians excepted, are represented. All the Byzantine churches of the Levant are present, though the Slav churches, except for some of their American branches, have remained aloof. (Political conditions explain this position in great part.) The Copts, Ethiopians, Nestorians, and Jacobites have their place, even though it be not conspicuous. The Old Catholics and Polish National Church are there, but not highly influential. The extreme rightist and leftist churches of Protestantism have not yet joined the Council.

In other words, the solid core of the Council is formed at present by the middle-of-the-stream churches of the Protestant tradition. Nor are these churches homogeneous in their attitudes. Some are chiefly orientated toward evangelical witness and collaboration with varying degrees of indifference to doctrinal orthodoxy. Others are developing a feeling for tradition which gives them rightist leanings in theology. In spite of the presence of the Orientals, the Council looks more like a middle-Protestant enterprise than a really universal get-together of Christians. In fact, one might ask without malice if the name, World Council of Churches, is not a little too pretentious at the moment for the concrete fact it labels.

(c) *Structure*

The World Council is a fellowship as described by the first article of its constitution. This fellowship acts with ultimate authority through its Assembly, which is a quinquennial congress of the delegates chosen by the churches who are the constituent members of the Council. The delegates may be clerical or lay, male or female. The number of delegates for each church is determined by the Assembly for the subsequent Assembly. This number is not set definitively, but the constitution indicates that the Assembly should strive for equality of representation, bearing in mind the numerical membership of the member churches, their geographical distribution and confessional pluralism.

The last meeting of the Assembly was at Evanston in 1954 and according to the constitution the next one should be in 1959, but it will be held in 1960 somewhere in the Far East.

The continuation agent of the Assembly is the Central Committee, which acts for the Assembly when it is not in session. All members of the Presidium, who are never more than six, belong to the Committee, whose maximum number is ninety, all chosen by the Assembly. The Presidium is the staff of the presiding chairmen of the Assembly and all have the title of president, but they are not empowered to be executives or heads of the Central Committee, which elects its own chairman. The Committee meets once a year at a place it chooses. In 1956 it met in Budapest, and in 1957 at Yale University, U.S.A.

Since this group is not in session continuously, there is an Executive Committee of the Central Committee. All the members of the Presidium are members of this Executive Committee along with the chairman and vice-chairman of the Central Committee and twelve other members of the Central Committee, elected by the Committee. The General Secretary of the Council is also the secretary of the Executive Committee. At the present moment he is Dr. Willem Adolf Visser't Hooft, of Holland, who belongs to the Dutch Reformed Church. He has held his post since the founding of the Council and he has long been one of the leading figures of the ecumenical movement. His piety, skill, patience, and understanding have been largely responsible for the smooth-running of the Council and it might not be too rash to say that he is the dynamo of the great organization.

The General Secretary and his staff of assistants are the standing executive organ of the Council and its general committees. The seat of the secretariat is 17 Route de Malegnou, Geneva, Switzerland. (The World Council is incorporated under Swiss law.)

The Council also has standing commissions for the diverse tasks entrusted by the Assembly or Central Committee.[9] One of the important commissions is that of Faith and Order with its permanent secretariat at Council headquarters in Geneva. This commission existed before the foundation of the Council and was instrumental in its formation. However, it is not unsafe to say that the Council chiefly took over the activities of the Conference on Life and Work, which in its new form absorbed Faith and Order, leaving it however with its own constitution.[10] Thus the Lund Conference, which was the third meeting of the Conference on Faith and Order, was held in 1952 after the foundation of the World Council. Likewise, the Oberlin North American study conference of 1957 was a Faith and Order enterprise.[10a] There is some ambivalence in the status of Faith and Order. It is definitely and enthusiastically a part of the World Council, of which it is a constituent commission, but somehow it retains a life of its own. How its relative autonomy will develop in the future is not so clear, though its present activities are vibrant and fruitful. Until the fall of 1957, the American Methodist, Dr. J. Robert Nelson, was secretary of the Commission. After he became dean of the Divinity School of Vanderbilt University, Dr. Keith Bridston, another American, took over the post.

One of the interesting structural elements of the Council

is the "Ecumenical Institute" at the Château de Bossey on Lake Geneva, not far from the World Council headquarters. It is a center of studies where leaders of the ecumenical movement are formed through courses of study and discussions. The Council also has its own periodical organs: *The Ecumenical Review* (a quarterly), *The Ecumenical Press Service* (weekly), both published from Geneva. The United States Conference of the World Council publishes the *Ecumenical Courier* (bimonthly) from New York.

(d) *Activities*

According to the constitution, the World Council is a continuation of the previous Life and Work, Faith and Order movements. In the practical order it facilitates the common action of the churches by being the meeting point of all. In the order of theory it promotes cooperative study. In all of its activities its central concern is to develop the ecumenical consciousness of the churches. In line with this activity it establishes relations with denominational federations of world-wide scope.

Although through information and intermediation the Council supports the churches in their missionary activity, the prime function of the Council is to organize world conferences on specific subjects where discussion and the publication of such discussion will be the immediate fruit. For the concrete tasks involved in such discussions, commissions are appointed to further the work which the Assembly, because of its large numbers and short life, cannot accomplish.

Here again mention must be made of the constituent commission of Faith and Order. This enterprise, even before the existence of the Council, was anxious to bring about unity of the churches on the basis of theory and theology. It is therefore the chief dogmatic organ of the Council in the study of questions on faith, order, and worship. Such study cannot help but be theological and the commission is a theologian's enterprise. However, it is not merely a group interested in all or any theological questions. It is always oriented to the question of the unity of the Church, and whatever theology it engages in will be related to that primary question.

The other commissions, some twelve in number, deal with problems of finance, information, missionary activity, youth programs, refugees, etc. The Council is also in touch with the organization of United Nations through its Commission of the Churches on International Affairs.

2. THE PAST

From the brief outline of the Council given above, it is clear that it did not suddenly burst forth full-panoplied from the head of Jove. It is the logical outcome of earlier efforts. In the history of the ecumenical movement edited by Rouse and Neill, the different threads which have intertwined to form the present Council are traced back to the sixteenth century.[11] To do a similar work here is out of the question. Let us simplify by stating that the Council rose ultimately because of the work of three men of recent times. Needless to say, they were not alone and others could, even should be mentioned, but these three stand out in a peculiar way. The men are Dr. John Raleigh Mott (Methodist layman, American, 1865–1955), Bishop Charles Henry Brent (Episcopal, Canadian-American, 1862–1929), and Archbishop Nathan Söderblom (Lutheran, Swedish, 1866–1931).

John R. Mott (who died in Florida on January 31, 1955) while a student at Cornell University listened to the British evangelist, J. E. K. Studd, and decided to dedicate his life to the Christian cause. After his graduation in 1888, he became General Secretary of the Student Y.M.C.A. in America. He was also interested in the Student Christian Movement, which was spreading all over Europe and America. This movement was missionary in its aspiration, and so the missions became a permanent loving concern for Mott. He organized the movement by founding the World's Student Christian Federation at a meeting at Vadstena, Sweden, in 1895. Because of his missionary interests, he traveled widely in the East and West and was chairman of the Edinburgh World Missionary Conference in 1910. This latter meeting was most important, because it was the first large Protestant interdenominational congress. It influenced Bishop Brent, and Mott personally influenced Archbishop Söderblom.

Mott became chairman of the International Missionary Council, which was conceived at Edinburgh and came to full existence in 1921. He headed its meetings at Jerusalem (1928), and Tambaram, India (1938), but retired from this position in 1941 and consequently did not chair the Whitby, Canada, meeting of 1948. He also entered wholeheartedly into the work of the Conference on Life and Work and was the chairman of the Oxford meeting in 1937. His merits were recognized both at Amsterdam and Evanston, for both Assemblies elected him honorary (and supernumerary) president of the Council. He was also awarded the Nobel Peace Prize in 1946.

The life of Dr. Mott brought together in one man three international and interdenominational associations: the

Y.M.C.A.; the Student Christian Movement, which was consolidated into the World's Student Christian Federation; and the International Missionary Alliance. These three societies were the first attempts at large unions of Christian groups across national and denominational lines. From the success of their activities, the idea of a union of all the churches was not only powerfully suggested but lost the utopian glow which surrounded the efforts to realize it in earlier times.

This is evident in the history of Bishop Brent. As Bishop of the American Protestant Episcopal Church in the Philippine Islands, he saw the confusion and scandal produced by the divisions of Christianity. In the missions there was reduplication of work, an alienating bewilderment in the minds of the non-Christians on hearing conflicting conceptions of Christianity, and bitterness between the missionaries who should have been united in the charity which led them to the mission fields.

Brent attended Mott's World Missionary Conference of 1910 at Edinburgh, which was the birth of the International Missionary Council. But because of Brent something more came from it. The harmony and zeal of the Edinburgh meeting impressed him deeply. It showed him that cooperation across denominational lines was possible and he urged the Edinburgh delegates to work for a greater and more intimate union than was achieved at the congress. He himself on his voyage back to the Philippines attended the Cincinnati General Convention of the American Episcopal Church in 1910. He spoke glowingly of the Edinburgh experience and expressed his opinion that the time had come to bring the churches together in order to discuss their notions of faith and order. The opinion was rendered effective by the decision of the Convention to form a commission in order to organize a conference of the Christian communions all over the world to discuss faith and order. The First World War prevented an early realization of the meeting, and the atmosphere of distrust following the conflict delayed it more. However, the work of study and preformation for the congress went on, and it was greatly helped by the founding of the League of Nations, which gave the churches a stimulating pattern for their own union. Finally, at Lausanne, Switzerland, in 1927, the Conference on Faith and Order was assembled, consisting of 394 delegates and a staff of twelve. They represented 108 churches, principally from Europe and America. Brent was elected president but his bad health made him refuse the chairmanship of the Conference. Archbishop Söderblom of Uppsala was active and influential in the meeting. The Conference, in spite of the notions of some of its members, did not wish to form a united church. It wished only to see clearly the doctrinal differences which prevented such a union. The conference gathered to meet and ventilate differences, not to reconcile them for the moment. A Continuation Committee was appointed with Bishop Brent as chairman, and it met annually. In 1930 a second conference was projected, to be held not later than 1937. It was held in the August of that year at Edinburgh, but Bishop Brent had died almost ten years earlier and Archbishop Söderblom had passed away in 1931.

In the same year of 1937 but in July, the Conference of Life and Work met at Oxford, England. Some of the delegates at this meeting were also delegates at Edinburgh. The Archbishop of Canterbury, William Temple (1881–1944), a giant of the ecumenical movement, arranged a service in

St. Paul's, London, for the delegates of both conferences. The service acted as the climax of the Oxford meeting and the prelude for Edinburgh.

The two conferences united in a more conspicuous way. Each under the suggestion of members who had previously met independently for the purpose, appointed a committee of seven members and seven alternates, who were to work with a similar committee of the other Conference to found a World Council of Churches. (The name was proposed by Dr. Samuel McCrea Cavert, then president of the American Federation of Churches.) The new Council was to take over the work of the two conferences, which would then be dissolved. The Committee of Fourteen, as it was called, laid the groundwork for the foundation of the Council. The endeavor was halted by the appearance of the Second World War, but brought forth the Amsterdam Assembly of 1948.

Concerning the Faith and Order movement we have said something. It remains to say a little about the Conference of Life and Work. Just as the name of Bishop Brent is associated with Faith and Order, so Archbishop Nathan Söderblom is connected with Life and Work.

On the eve of the First World War in 1914 a group of churchmen met in Constance, Switzerland, but were forced to move to London, where they formed the World Alliance of Churches for Promoting International Peace. At Berne in the following year, 1915, its name was changed to the World Alliance for Promoting International Friendship through the Churches. It was also in 1914 that Nathan Söderblom, an ardent promoter of peace and later Nobel Peace Prize winner in 1930, was made Archbishop of Uppsala. In his efforts at reconciliation he had his eye on the World Alliance. The Archbishop worked hard to establish and maintain contact with church leaders everywhere and he had in mind a meeting of all. The World Alliance actually organized such a meeting at Oud Wassenaar (Holland), in 1919, at which Söderblom was prominent. It was the time in which the League of Nations had just been born, and Söderblom proposed a conference of the churches with the hope of forming something similar. This was really the germ of the Conference of Life and Work. The germ became a seed in the 1920 Geneva meeting of those who followed Söderblom's lead. There a committee was organized to arrange for a world conference, and took the name of the Universal Conference of the Church of Christ on Life and Work. The name was modified a year later to become the Universal Christian Conference on Life and Work.

Life and Work had a different orientation toward union than Faith and Order. The latter believed that no union could be achieved without the previous achievement of a doctrinal union of some kind. Söderblom believed that union was necessary now, and that the path of doctrinal discussion was too long to permit the union in our time. Hence he believed that union should be accomplished first and doctrinal differences ironed out in function of an existing union. With time, doctrinal questions did come up in Life and Work, nor could they be evaded. Yet it is largely true that Life and Work had less dogmatic preoccupations than its sister conference.

Life and Work had its first great assembly in Stockholm, 1925, with 600 delegates from 37 countries. The soul of the enthusiastic congress was Archbishop Söderblom. The meeting thus preceded the Lausanne meeting of Faith and Order of 1927, though Faith and Order was an older movement. The Conference met again after the death of Söderblom at Oxford, England, with John R. Mott in the chair. As we have seen, this conference prepared the way for its own absorption into the World Council. In the year of the birth of the World Council, the World Alliance, parent of Life and Work, voted its own extinction.

The other international organizations like the Y.M.C.A., the Y.W.C.A., World's Christian Student Federation, and International Missionary Council, have kept their own independence but they work in harmony and collaboration with the World Council.

Thus in few words was the World Council born out of the events of the recent past.

3. THE FUTURE

It is always safer to prophesy after the event. However, for some situations of tomorrow simple prognoses are possible even today. The World Council of Churches, which now solidifies the ecumenical movement stirring throughout the non-Catholic world, is a very young organization, not quite ten years old. Its features have not yet hardened nor has any dominating tendency been revealed.

One thing is evident, as can be gathered from the men and women who are engaged in the enterprise, and from the literature emanating from it. There is zeal, fervor, and great hope bubbling in World Council activities. Protestants of all denominations, Byzantine Orientals, and Old Catholics give spontaneous witness to the piety and charity palpable at World Council gatherings. Hope is the great emotion dynamizing the movement.

Is this hope founded on something more tangible than the easy recognition of the obvious good which would result from a more intimate church-union? Yes. The World Council is an evident proof that the churches can unite; for they have done so. However, the hope itself shows that more is expected. What can be expected?

The logic of the movement points to the *una sancta* as the goal of its strivings. But unfortunately, the different groups within the Council are not agreed on what the *una sancta* is. The Byzantine Orientals obviously believe that it is their church, made up of sister churches sharing the same faith, the same order, and the same worship. The other churches must enter into this one church. Needless to say, this is hardly the view of the others, and the view of the Byzantines is in a slight way an embarrassment for the total group, which in its vast majority entertains ideas quite alien to the Oriental position. The slight impact of the Old Catholics and Polish Nationals does not change this basic situation to any significant degree.

The majority of the members of the Council is split into two sides, though at the moment the split is neither painfully visible nor acutely troublesome. The two sides correspond roughly to the differing visions of Life and Work, and Faith and Order. What can be called the Life-and-Work-idea is the notion that the churches can immediately become one in spite of their doctrinal difficulties, which, if ignored for the moment, will in the light produced by union finally disappear. The opposite view is that doctrinal agreement must be achieved before the present association of the churches can more perfectly attain the unity of the *una sancta*.

These two opposing tendencies show up in different ways but they have not weakened the feelings of unity and of hope for the future. Whether they can continue in this anomalous existence is not too clear. It is certainly true that any desire, no matter how strong it be, must be ultimately disciplined by reality.

The believers in union-now are not united in their theologies. Some believe that dogmas and theories are not really of paramount importance. The experience of faith and the spirit of witness to the gospel are the essence of Christianity, while the theological formulation of it is accidental and variable. These are "undogmatic Christians," tolerant enough to allow theologians to ply their craft but not deeply concerned with their findings. Others are out-and-out indifferentists. One theology is as good as another— which is equivalent to saying that one is as bad as the other. The different theologies and creeds should not be a barrier to close union. In fact, "open communion" is what we need at once. The *Christian Century* (perhaps the most important Protestant journal in America, and strictly non-denominational in its structure and policy) with a note of exasperation criticized the diverse acts of worship at Evanston in 1954, where so many were "closed" to some degree. (The Byzantine Orientals gave communion only to Byzantines, and the Episcopalians only to those who were baptized and confirmed.) The whole postulate of the criticism was that "open communion" was needed at once if the World Council wished to live up to its claims of fellowship. This postulate is impatient of the idea of the relevancy of doctrine in so critical a move as one service of worship with "open communion" for all, when they are all so far apart in their conceptions of communion.

If this tendency should grow stronger in the Council, the churches will tend to become like religious orders in the Catholic Church—different modalities of life and worship implying no substantial difference, so that the member of one group could worship and communicate freely and legitimately in the services of the others. A closer union of churches would develop, but at the cost of the conviction of so many churches, namely, that their creed, code, and cult are warranted by the truth of the gospel, while others are not. It would make adherence to one church rather than another a matter of free personal preference; for in substance all are conceived as equally valid. This would dissolve sectarianism. But it would also shatter the basis on which sectarian fragmentation rests, which is a felt obligation to adhere strictly to the knowable will of Christ. The logical outcome of universal "open communion" will be the implicit confession of all the churches that they really had no substantial grounds for separating in the past, and that their separation today is in appearance rather than in fact.

Such an attitude is hard for many to adopt. They cannot relegate the question of truth to the indifferent impedimenta which collect in a marching soldier's knapsack. These believe that only on one theory can you have one church. Therefore, before the *una sancta* can become adequately visible in the Council, the churches must agree on doctrine. The present dogmatic basis, belief in Jesus Christ as God and Saviour, lays the point of departure for fruitful discussion in order to achieve more. It cannot be accepted as the last and final formula of union.

Those who think in this way are divided in their approaches to a richer formula. There are the constructionists, who think that Christians are antecedently uncommitted in the task of formulating a creed which can found true union. Hence, they would like to have the different churches freely construct a common creed by common consent in the light of desirability, rather than by investigation into normative origins.

Then there are those who believe that there already is a consensus among the churches on matters of doctrine. This consensus can be formulated and a common creed found. It need not be constructed, because it is there already. True, each church has something peculiar in its dogma, but a reduction to a least common denominator will be the Christian belief in which all are united. I wonder if Walter Horton's recent book, *Christian Theology: An Ecumenical Approach,*[12] is not a manifestation of this tendency.

Finally, there is a group which believes that collaborative research into the sources of Christian belief, patiently and impartially made, will give the indubitable creed which is the faith of the *una sancta*. When this faith has been found, the churches, because of their loyalty to Christ, will all accept it and divisions will disappear. Many an Anglican entertains this hope.

If the tendency represented by those who put unity in doctrine as the prerequisite for vital union of the churches takes on momentum, the World Council will for some time be a theological seminar of vast proportions, with a single church presumably emerging at the end.

In the light of the present it can be prudently said that neither tendency can take over the Council. If either group would succeed, the other would have to secede, and both are anxious to avoid secession, which would annul all the good which has already been won.

Hence, coexistence and compromise will be the mood prevailing in Council meetings of the immediate future. Now such a tactic will favor the union-now champions. To a Catholic, who would spontaneously see the problem as the Faith and Order people see it, this is regrettable. Visser't Hooft has recognized this Catholic sympathy but points out that it arises from the fact that Catholics cannot see that the warm union already forged is of great help in the solution of dogmatic aporias for the future.[13] Since the Council is not the final solution of the problem of separation but only its first step, doctrinal unity is not the task of the moment. Being together, praying together, discussing together is the best beginning for being one eventually. At the moment the Council has no theology and no ecclesiology. In fact, since the Council is not the Church, nor a church, there is no reason why it should have any.

These observations are just enough. However, just as the negation of the validity and relevance of metaphysics is a metaphysical stand, so the refusal to make an ecclesiological commitment is really an ecclesiological stand. It is the stand of those who believe that the ecclesiological enterprise is either baneful or irrelevant to the life and work of the Church. In other words, the non-dogmatic wing of Christians will set the tone of the Council; for their position must be accepted by the Council as a point of departure. That they will be converted to the views of their opponents is most unlikely; for they will get stronger as the Council cedes more and more to their persuasions. By ignoring the supposition of those who believe that unity of belief is the first task, the Council, practically though not by formal theory, is accepting the ecclesiology of the anti-ecclesiologists.

If this analysis be correct, the Council of the future is going to grow more and more activist. The question of truth will recede more and more from the minds of those engaged in its work. Anglo-Saxon pragmatism will be the melting force fusing the elements together. Those elements which resist this force will naturally be left outside of the fusion.

In other words, if the truth-first defenders are not converted, they will eventually have to withdraw. If they do, the World Council will have failed in its hope, though it will have united a great segment of the Protestant churches of the world. It will be a partial union reducing the manifold of churches into fewer groups, but the remainder will be more irreducible than ever. I do hope that no one will see hostility in this sober and calm opinion.

★ 2 ★

Catholic Ecumenism

I. CURRENT ACTIVITIES

That the Catholic Church is ecumenical-minded needs no proof. It is just as obvious that its ecumenism is different from that represented by the World Council of Churches. At the actual moment there are different Catholic ecumenical projects at work.

1. There are religious congregations and communities primarily dedicated to the reunion of all Christians. In this country we have the Friars of the Atonement (At-one-ment), founded by Father Paul James Francis (Lewis Thomas Wattson, 1863–1940).[14] This religious congregation was founded in 1898 as an Anglican community while Father Paul was an Episcopalian priest. The rule of the community, as well as for the women's branch of it, was Franciscan. In 1909 both communities were received into the Catholic Church, retaining their corporate existence.

Father Paul was primarily devoted to the unity of Christians. Under the stimulus of a letter from Rev. Spencer Jones, an English leader of the Anglo-Catholic movement, Father Paul founded the Octave of Prayer for Christian Unity. This he propagated throughout his life, beginning in 1907 before his community was Catholic. His objective was the dedication of the days between the feast of St. Peter's Chair at Rome and the feast of the Conversion of St. Paul (January 18–25) to prayer for reunion. The Octave of Chris-

[29]

tian Unity was blessed by St. Pius X, and Pope Benedict XV made it an official prayer of the Church. It spread all over the Catholic world and was used outside of the Catholic communion by Anglicans and Orientals. The Society of the Atonement, Father Paul's congregation, promotes this Octave in our day, and it is now called the Chair of Unity Octave. This work is directed in America by Fr. Edward F. Hanahoe, S.A. Msgr. Paul Couturier of Lyons, France (1881–1953), promoted this campaign of prayer, with a change of accent, so that non-Catholics could accept it without being repelled by the frankly pro-papal note of the official prayers. In Couturier's form the Octave is celebrated by many non-Catholics in our time.

At Chevetogne, Belgium, there exists the Benedictine Priory of Union. It was originally founded by Dom Lambert Beauduin (b. 1873) at Amay, Belgium, in 1926 and translated to its present site, Chevetogne, in 1939. This monastery was first interested mainly in the reunion of the Orientals with the Western Church. However, its interests include all the churches and its principal contribution is *Irénikon,* a quarterly review in French founded in 1927. This review is highly esteemed by Catholics and non-Catholics alike. Non-Catholics appreciate very much the sympathetic slant given to their activities.

2. With headquarters in Rome, the Unitas association under the guidance of Father Charles Boyer, S.J., strives for the reunion of non-Catholics with the Catholic Church. The association, founded in 1945, has its Central Committee in Rome, with affiliate groups spread internationally and organized into diocesan units. It publishes its quarterly, *Unitas,* in three languages: Italian from Rome; French from Paris; English from Graymoor, New York. The English

edition is directed by the Atonement Friars, who collaborate closely with Unitas. Formal membership in this association is restricted to Catholics but it has many non-Catholic friends. Fr. Boyer has long been engaged in the ecumenical movement, even though non-Catholic ecumenists are divided in their estimation of his work.

Under the secretaryship of Prof. Dr. J. G. M. Willebrands, of the Philosophicum, Warmond, Holland, the Catholic Oecumenical Conference, founded in 1952, holds annual meetings for the discussion of ecumenical questions. The Conference holds its annual meeting in different places, to which recognized scholars and leaders of Catholic ecumenism are invited. The findings of the meetings are then communicated in reports to those who are interested in the work.

The German Una Sancta movement is the best-known Catholic endeavor in the reunion effort. After the First World War the need of the union of Christians was felt in different circles of Germany. The general mood was labeled the Una Sancta Movement, in which the Protestants Friedrich Heiler and Friedrich Sigmund Schultze were prominent. (Both together founded the current *Oekumenische Einheit,* a non-Catholic ecumenical periodical published in Munich, Germany.) The mood originally was ambiguous but was finally orientated by a scintillating figure, the German Catholic priest, Dr. Josef Max Metzger (1887–1944).[15] This man, a chaplain of the German Army in the First World War, returned to Germany a convinced pacifist. He strove to create the friendship of all men for each other and in his campaign he recognized the need of religious union. At Graz in 1919 he founded a religious institute, with male and female branches, called the Society of Christ

the King of the White Cross, whose members were devoted
to Christian love exercised among the poor, the lowly, the
outcasts, and disinherited. He himself, as Brother Paul, was
austere in his own life, abstaining from alcohol, meats, and
tobacco, according to the rule of his congregation. Seeing
the Una Sancta a real mood but unorganized, after contact
with many people of his own land and beyond, of his own
Church and beyond, he traversed Germany on lecture tours.
Finally, in 1939, he organized the Una Sancta Confraternity.
Metzger's pacifism, internationalism, and prophetic angular-
ity drew the eye of the Nazis on him. Since in his later
years the scene of his labors was Berlin itself, he was a
closely watched man. It is no wonder that he finally was
condemned to beheading as a traitor in the last years of the
war. His death, which was not exactly a martyrdom for
Una Sancta, though his work in that organization was held
against him by his judges, made a kind of romantic image
of him, and the image abides.

Dr. Metzger's work was continued by Dr. Matthias
Laros, but the name has been changed. It is now the Una
Sancta Union and it has its headquarters in Metzger's old
center, the House of Christ the King, at Meitingen near
Augsburg, Germany. At first Laros also directed Metzger's
Rundbriefe, which now appear as *Una Sancta,* a quarterly
published by the Kyrios Verlag, Meitingen, directed by
Dom Thomas Sartory, O.S.B., of the Niederalteich Abbey.

Just after the Second World War the Una Sancta was
a thriving and lively organization indeed. Everywhere its
groups were active in discussions and meetings. However,
in the last years it has lost much of its vibrancy, because
interest in it seems to have died down.

The peculiarity of the Una Sancta movement is that

[32]

it does not try to make converts of non-Catholics. It wishes rather to form an atmosphere of friendliness and mutual understanding. The dynamism of the whole effort is confidence in God, who alone can make of many one. If the Christians live up to their vocation of love and mutual affection, then God's power will take over. Concerning Metzger's own absolute faith in the Church and the necessity of belonging to her, there can be no doubt. However, he did not think that a proselytizing approach to the non-Catholic would be beneficial. He wished rather to have Catholic and non-Catholic speak to each other from the heart, so that each could see what the other stood for, and in seeing it recognize that they were nearer to each other than they thought.

Indirectly influenced by the Metzger movement must be mentioned another German group, small but very significant. It numbers some twenty-five members altogether, who roughly half and half are Catholics and Lutherans. The group is quite nameless, though many of the Lutheran section are members of the high-church *Michaelsbruder-schaft*. The Catholic members work under the patronage of Archbishop Lorenz Jaeger of Paderborn. They are an outstanding group, including the dynamic church-historian, Prof. Josef Lortz, formerly of the University of Münster and now at the University of Mainz; Dr. Robert Grosche of Cologne; Fr. Hugh Rahner, S.J., of Innsbruck; and the layman, Prof. Josef Pieper, of the University of Münster.

This group meets annually in different places, the hosts alternating, so that one meeting is under a Catholic chairmanship and the following under Lutheran. The discussions are strictly theological and historical, for which all the members are well prepared. If the extent of the activity is not so impressive, the solidity of its membership leaves nothing to be desired.

3. In addition to the ecumenical reviews already mentioned, three more must be added. One of the most respected is *Istina* (Russian word for truth). This quarterly review in French is edited from Boulogne-sur-Seine by the well-known Dominican ecumenist, Fr. C.-J. Dumont. It began in 1954 as an extension of the monthly bulletin of the *Istina* study center which appears as *Vers l'unité chrétienne*. *Istina*, as its title in Russian indicates, is especially interested in the Russian Orthodox, but its scope is wider and includes the whole reunion issue. Fr. Dumont and his work are highly admired by non-Catholic ecumenists.

In English we have the twelve-year-old *Eastern Churches Quarterly*, edited by Dom Bede Winslow, O.S.B., of St. Augustine's Abbey, Ramsgate, England, in collaboration with Donald Attwater. Both of these men are well known, especially for their studies and research into the life and thought of the Eastern Churches. Their review deals primarily with Oriental Christianity, but also includes all ecumenical concerns.

Though *Herder-Korrespondenz*, a general monthly published by the Herder Verlag of Freiburg, Breisgau, is not strictly an ecumenical review, yet it sedulously carries ecumenical news and comment. Dr. Karlheinz Schmidthüs, in charge of this work, is intensely interested and well informed in the field.

2. ECCLESIASTICAL NORMS

Canon law obviously carries principles which will guide the Catholic interested in ecumenical work, which simply is work for the reunion of all Christians into one Church. The application of such principles sometimes is difficult, because the circumstances to which the application must be made are quite new. This happened in the field of ecumenical action. Hence, four Roman pronouncements directly bearing on the ecumenical movement authoritatively apply canon law to the question. They are the Response of the Holy Office of July 8, 1927; the Encyclical of Pius XI, *Mortalium animos;* the Monitum of the Holy Office of 1948; and the Instruction of the Holy Office of 1949.

The first document was the result of the first meetings of Life and Work, and Faith and Order. Dr. Henry A. Atkinson, General Secretary for Life and Work, went personally to Rome to invite the Catholic Church to the Stockholm meeting of 1925. He was received courteously but no response was given to his invitation. Archbishop Söderblom later received a refusal to the invitation to attend the Conference. A committee for Faith and Order visited Pope Benedict XV as early as 1919 to extend an invitation to the Catholic Church to take part in the Lausanne Conference. In 1926 Bishop Brent went personally for the same purpose. On both occasions the persons were received with courtesy and friendliness but the invitation was clearly refused. On July 8, 1927, the Holy Office issued a response to a question sent to or formulated by it. The question was: "May Catholics take part in or promote (*favere*) congresses, meetings, lectures, or societies which have the scope of uniting into a religious confederation all who in any sense whatever call themselves Christians?"[16] To this general and wide question an unconditioned "no" was given, and reference was made to the rejection of a similar question in 1919 based on the prohibition of participation in the nineteenth-century English Association for the Promotion of the Unity of Christendom.[17]

However, we must also quote from the document given to the 1919 committee for the Lausanne Conference. The document, after stating the impossibility of the Church's participation in the Conference, says:

> His Holiness, however, by no means wishes to disapprove of the Congress in question for those who are not in union with the Chair of Peter; on the contrary, he earnestly desires and prays that, if the Congress is practicable, those who take part in it may, by the grace of God, see the light and become reunited to the visible head of the Church, by whom they will be received with open arms.[18]

On January 6, the Feast of the Epiphany, 1928, Pius XI issued the Encyclical, *Mortalium animos,* the most extended and most solemn treatment of the ecumenical movement as it was embodied in Life and Work, and Faith and Order.[19] In this pronouncement the Pope forbade all participation in the movement, which he calls "panchristian." The reasons are: the postulates of the union deny that the *una sancta* already visibly exists in our world and affirm that she must be brought into existence; it is implicitly affirmed that union can be achieved without unity of doctrine; the Catholic Church is not considered to be the Church of Christ but one of many communities in that Church, which is not coextensive with her. These postulates involve relativism of dogma, modernism in theology, and indifferentism in ecclesiology. Any meeting or association based on such principles contradicts the total faith of Catholicism, so that no Catholic can in logic or charity take part in them.

As we have seen in our outline of the history of the ecumenical movement, many changes have taken place within it. How does the Church stand on the World Council? In 1948, on June 5, shortly before the aborning Council met in Amsterdam, the Holy Office issued an admonition (*monitum*). It is short, so we shall give an English rendition of it here:

It has been learned that in various places, contrary to the prescriptions of the sacred canons, and without leave of the Holy See, mixed congresses of Catholics and non-Catholics have been held, wherein matters of faith have been discussed. Let all remember, in accord with canon 1325 §3, that it is prohibited to take part in these congresses without the forementioned permission. This holds for the laity and clergy, both secular and religious. Much less is it permitted for Catholics to convoke or organize such congresses. The ordinaries, therefore, must urgently see to it that all observe these prescriptions strictly.

The obligation to observe these prescriptions is even greater in the case of "ecumenical" congresses, as they are called, in which Catholics, be they either lay or clerical, may not in any way take part without previous consent of the Holy See.

In the congresses described and elsewhere, common services of worship have often been held. All are again admonished that it is absolutely forbidden by canons 1258 and 731 §2 to take part in common services of worship.

Given at Rome, from the quarters of the Holy Office, June 5, 1948.

Peter Vigorita, Notary.[20]

At Amsterdam there were different categories of participants in the sessions: (1) delegates, (2) alternates, (3) consultants, (4) fraternal delegates, (5) observers, (6) accredited visitors, (7) youth delegates.[21] This arrangement became a matter of rule at Amsterdam and was adopted without change at Evanston. Many Catholics had indicated to the Amsterdam Assembly their desire to attend, but the Monitum above given made it necessary for all to apply to Rome. No permission was given to anyone, though Fr. Charles Boyer was present in the city of Amsterdam during the sessions and engaged in conversations with the delegates personally. Likewise, Catholic newspaper reporters attended the meetings, but of course they were in no formal way participants of the Assembly.

The Monitum lays down a general principle which it did not invent but found in ancient and modern canon law, namely, that a religious fusion of Catholic and non-Catholic is impossible. This is especially true in the matter of worship. The Monitum also recognized that meeting the non-Catholic in terms of religious concern was not necessarily religious fusion. What is more, such a meeting might be good. It then solved the problem of what is sheer meeting and what is fusion not theoretically but by the practical instrument of law. The decision whether a concrete gathering, including Catholics, is religious fusion or mere meeting belongs to ecclesiastical authority and not to the individual Catholic. Hence, if the Catholic on his own initiative wishes for good purposes to attend a concrete gathering, he must consult the authorities, who will judge practically but decisively whether this implies religious fusion with non-Catholics or mere meeting where good fruit can be expected. It was not excluded from the realm of practical possibility that Catholics meet non-Catholics in religious discussion, but it was affirmed that this was not to be done without the approbation of competent authority. All these principles are so traditionally Catholic that they are taken for granted by anyone who knows what Catholicism is.

The Monitum was too jejune to answer all the questions suggested by it. That the World Council was involved was clear enough from the timing of the document. Did it also include in its gaze the Una Sancta Confraternity? Did it forbid every kind of intellectual discussion between Catholics and non-Catholics? Interpretations were being given by many but something more authoritative was required. It came on December 20, 1949, with the Instruction of the Holy Office, *Ecclesia catholica*.[22]

The Catholic Church takes no actual part in "ecumenical" conventions and other assemblies of a similar character. Yet, as numerous pontifical statements show, she has, despite this fact, never ceased nor will she ever cease to pursue with deepest concern and promote with assiduous prayers to God every endeavor to bring about what was so close to the heart of Christ the Lord, viz., that all who believe in Him "may be made perfect in one" (Jn 17:23).

The Instruction goes on to state its meaning. The unity conceived is the unity of the Catholic Church, and reunion means the acceptance of Catholicism by non-Catholic Christians. There is no equivocation here and no ambiguity. However, with reference to current non-Catholic ecumenism, the Instruction says that this is a joy to Catholics and "an inducement to lend their assistance to all who are sincerely seeking the truth, by entreating light and strength for them from God in fervent prayer." What is more, the desire for reunion in non-Catholic ecumenical efforts is not to be explained merely by external events and cultural changes; for it has been awakened "under the inspiring grace of God."

Concerning the "assistance" to be given to dissident Christians the Instruction wishes to speak. It states that some past efforts have not rested on correct principles. In consequence the Instruction indicates the principles to be followed:

1. Reunion activities are the proper function of the bishops; for they are the pastors and teachers of the flock. Bishops are admonished to know what is going on in their dioceses and establish centers with trained priests for the work of information.

2. In all conversations with non-Catholics the Catholic doctrine must be given in its entirety. There must be no slurring over unliked dogmas nor the use of misleading expressions for genuine doctrine in order to cater to the credal prejudices of non-Catholics. Such devices are deceitful and raise hopes in non-Catholics which can never be fulfilled.

3. In addition to the ordinary media of information— lectures, information centers, books, pamphlets, etc.—the bishops may contemplate the use of interdenominational reunions. Concerning these the 1948 Monitum was framed. These are of different kinds. One category is not ecumenical at all; for it is the collaboration of Catholics and non-Catholics in the defense of the natural law and basic Christian doctrine against the attacks of the common enemy. This is a cultural enterprise and not directly religious. The Monitum did not legislate for such meetings, and the remarks made in the Instruction imply approbation for such projects, in accord with the repeated pronouncements of Pope Pius XII.

Concerning civic collaboration of Catholics with non-Catholics the Instruction is not concerned. It does have in mind two other forms of mixed gatherings: the open intercredal meeting or congress and the closed theological colloquy. The open meeting is not a Catholic lecture where non-Catholics can in a question period propose non-Catholic difficulties. Such lectures are not contemplated by the Monitum or the Instruction. The open meeting, for many or few, is a gathering constructed to bring together Catholics and non-Catholics in order to discuss their credal views and differences on a basis of equality and reciprocal freedom. The theological colloquy is of the same kind but restricted to representative theologians of different denominations. In this second kind of meeting the number and quality of the participants excludes a general public.

These kinds of reunions are the object of the Monitum's directives and of the Instruction's concern. It neither approves of them in general nor does it disapprove of them. They are capable of good, because they give the Catholics an opportunity to give effective witness to their faith. They also involve a danger, because indifferentism and fusionism can result in Catholics who attend.

Since there is an ambiguity in such meetings, the bishops must weigh the probable benefits and evils resulting from the gatherings. If the ordinaries prudently think that the results will be mainly good, such meetings can be organized with or without the collaboration of non-Catholic associations. However, such organization ultimately belongs to the bishop alone. No one else may plan or organize such meetings or conventions without previous authorization of the bishop. What is more, the bishop must exercise constant vigilance over the meetings. If disorientation of

Catholics is probable, the Catholics must not be allowed to attend indiscriminately, and if in the progress of the conference unwelcome trends show up, the bishop must use means to end the sessions, immediately or gradually.

For the theological colloquies the Catholic representatives must be chosen in the light of their scholarship and evident allegiance to the Church and her norms. They must be priests.

4. For three years from the date of the publication of the Instruction (1950), all bishops have the faculty to organize or approve meetings of the kind described. Three conditions are, however, imposed. (*a*) There must be no interdenominational services of liturgical worship. (*b*) All activities of the meetings must be episcopally supervised. (*c*) A yearly report must be sent to the Holy Office describing the number of meetings held and what occurred in them. This three-year faculty, according to common canonical practice, is presumably renewable on request. The faculty is only applicable to mixed meetings which are local to the diocese. Interdiocesan, national, or international meetings cannot be planned and organized without previous consent of the Holy See.

5. By common worship something more than common prayer is understood. The opening and closing of the sessions with prayers approved by the Church are not to be construed as common worship.

6. Ecumenical work and intercredal discussion is the exclusive function of the ordinary. It is well if the bishops of a region work together and establish regional or national organizations for the work.

7. Religious are admonished to obey the directives of the Instruction. They are subject to the local ordinaries

in this matter. The exempt religious, in consequence, are not free to prescind from the authority of the local bishop in their ecumenical efforts.

The Monitum and the implementing Instruction form one body of directives. Though dogmatic principles are implicit in the pronouncements, they are formally disciplinary in scope. Consequently, there is no question here of "definitions." We are given decisions for the practical order, and of course the practical order is always changing, so that the decisions of the moment are also capable of being replaced by new ones.

Moralists and canonists are the proper persons to interpret the documents given. The dogmatic theologian can find dogmatic guidance and data in the decrees, but this he will do according to theological method in order to achieve speculative truth. Law and dogma are related but they must not be identified. Propositions legitimately or illegitimately deduced from a theological analysis of the directives do not produce disciplinary obligation. The law as law creates obligation, and the authentic interpreter of law is episcopal regimen, primatial or local. The opinions of canonists will be helpful in further detailing the interpretations given by the episcopal pastors, but even they are not the authoritative interpreters of the law. That office belongs to the episcopate alone, either acting through the universal primate at Rome or through the local ordinary for his see.

One thing is easily gathered from the Roman decrees. They are concerned with interdenominational meetings sponsored wholly or in part by Catholics. The question of participation in conferences exclusively organized by non-Catholics is dismissed briefly at the very beginning of the

Instruction: "The Catholic Church takes no part in 'ecumenical' conventions and other assemblies of a similar character." No more is said, and the mind of the framers of the Instruction seems to be that no more need be said. Consequently, the possibility of formal participation in World Council activities is rejected by disciplinary principle. What is more, the principle is fundamental.

Let us see how the Holy Office itself understands its decree in the light of what it has done since the Instruction was published in 1950. Consequently, it is not pertinent to cite the fact that with ecclesiastical permission Fr. Metzger was an observer at the Lausanne meeting of Faith and Order in 1927, or that there were unofficial Catholic observers present by invitation at the Oxford meeting of the Conference of Life and Work in 1937, or that there were four priests and a layman present at the Conference of Faith and Order in Edinburgh in the same year.[23]

The first ecumenical meeting held after the publication of the Instruction was in Lund in 1952, where the third Conference of Faith and Order was held. This group, as we have seen, is also a constitutive committee of the World Council. At this meeting, in the category of "observers from the Roman Catholic Church," nominated by the Vicar Apostolic of Sweden, Bishop John Müller, four Catholics, residents of Sweden, were present,[24] three of whom can easily be recognized in the list of "Accredited Visitors" in the "Who's Who" of the Conference.[25] (One of them was a monsignor, B. Assarsson, and another was a Jesuit, Fr. Gerlach.) At the Oberlin North American study conference of Faith and Order in September, 1957, two Catholic priests, John Sheerin, C.S.P., and Gustave Weigel, S.J., were accredited but unofficial observers.

At Lund, Evanston, and Oberlin, Catholics were present as reporters for the press. No difficulty was offered to those people either by Rome or the local bishop. However, at Evanston, except for reporters, no Catholics were given permission to take part in any activity of the Council.

The Lund action shows that the unquestioned principle by which the Catholic Church, formally as such, will have no formal part in the work of the World Council does not in the Roman mind mean that there is no recognition of the Council or that she cannot in a completely neutral but friendly way have unofficial observers at the meetings, if the occasion favors such an action. It does, however, mean that officially the Catholic Church refuses any formal participation in Council activities. Outside of the meetings Catholic scholars and theologians can always be freely consulted by Council workers and their studies incorporated into Council findings.[26]

3. ECUMENICAL WRITINGS

"It is an impressive fact that the stream of Roman Catholic publications concerning ecumenical questions is still growing."[27] This is an observation of Dr. Willem Adolf Visser't Hooft, who keeps in contact with this growing literature and no doubt has secretaries who gather the material for him. Yet he does not wish to give an account of all that is being written, because of the quantity of it. Much less shall we attempt such a task here.

Let us see some of the more prominent works so far published. We have given the names of Father Paul, Metzger, Couturier, Boyer, Laros, Dumont, Sartory, Winslow, Attwater, Lortz, Rahner, Grosche, Willebrands, Hanahoe, and others. All of these men have written on the subject, but there are others who must also be mentioned. Max Pribilla, S.J., both in *Stimmen der Zeit* and elsewhere has published studies on ecumenism. His *Von der kirchlichen Einheit, Stockholm-Lausanne-Rom*[28] is considered by Catholics and non-Catholics as a good report of the earlier stages of the ecumenical movement. Yves Congar, O.P., is unquestionably one of the leading Catholic figures on ecumenism, and his *Divided Christendom* is known and generally well received.[29] The distinguished ecclesiologist, Charles Journet, years ago published *L'Union des églises et le christianisme.*[30] A. Rademacher's works are significant, and Karl Adam's small collection of three sermons, *The One and Holy,* caused great comment.[31] Charles Boyer's little *One Shepherd* and Matthias Laros' *Schöpferischer Friede der Konfessionen* are popular introductions to Catholic ecumenism, but of different tempers.[32]

In the article of Visser't Hooft whose first words headed this section, the author names and evaluates recent Catholic ecumenical works. He is critical of Msgr. Gustave Thils's *Histoire doctrinale du mouvement oecuménique,*[33] and though he admits its scholarly merits, he is not quite satisfied. He is rather dissatisfied with the Benedictine Thomas Sartory's *Die ökumenische Bewegung und die Einheit der Kirche,*[34] granting it, however, a core of sound knowledge. For Edward F. Hanahoe's *Catholic Ecumenism*[35] he has little admiration.

George Tavard, A.A., published a controverted little work, a compact condensation of information and theology, *The Catholic Approach to Protestantism.*[36] He criticized Fr. Hanahoe adversely, but he in turn has been reproached by Visser't Hooft for being too Catholic, and by Msgr. Joseph Fenton for not being Catholic enough.[37] If Fr. Hanahoe met with both Catholic and non-Catholic strictures, he nonetheless merited Fr. Boyer's judgment that his study gives the genuine Catholic doctrine in the matter.[38]

The last writer named by Visser't Hooft is the Belgian Jérôme Hamer, O.P., with specific reference to the latter's article in *Istina*.[39] Fr. Hamer deserves particular mention because the serenity and sympathetic spirit of his study of Protestantism, his solid knowledge of the field, and his perfect control of Catholic theological method place him high in the list of Catholic ecumenists.[40]

★ 3 ★

Theological Reflections

Visser't Hooft finds that Catholic ecumenists fall into two classes, and paradoxically the same man may be of both classes in different phases of his thought.[41] Some Catholics take an "outsider's" view of the Council, considering it something strange and disturbing. Others are capable of taking an "insider's" view of it; for, though as Catholics they do not participate in the Council, yet they existentially feel its élan for unity, and they realize that this impulse is the Catholic urge they themselves possess.

The General Secretary of the Council has put his finger precisely on the Catholic ambivalence in current ecumenical preoccupations. However, the ambivalence is not of the Catholic's making. Ecumenism, generically and abstractly, stands for a felt drive toward the reduction of all who use the Christian name into a unity corresponding to the *una sancta* of the Nicene symbol. As a concrete label of our day, ecumenism usually refers to the World Council in its central and peripherical reality.

With regard to ecumenism in its abstract and generic sense, the Catholic feels no ambivalence whatsoever. He wholeheartedly desires the union of all Christians, and even non-Christians, in the *una sancta*. What is more, he has a perfectly clear concept of what that Church is. It is for him concretely the Catholic Church, visibly centered in the jurisdictional and doctrinal primacy of the Bishop of Rome. Hence, the Catholic spontaneously identifies the Church with the Catholic Church without further distinction, although he must frequently add the word "Roman" to avoid all equivocation. By his faith he holds that the one Church of Christ presently exists, essentially perfect, and it is exclusively the Catholic Church, whose visible Catholicity from the day of Peter's death to our own time implies Roman centrality. He inevitably feels as an expression of his own conviction the stirring words of Augustine:

We must cling to the Christian religion and the fellowship of the Church which is catholic, and is called the Catholic Church not only by her own but by all her foes as well. Like it or not, even heretics and those fostered in schism call the Catholic Church by no other name than Catholic. The point is, they cannot be understood unless they specify her by that title which is the whole world's name for her.[42]

There are many things which with absolute justice keep me in the bosom of the Catholic Church. There is the consensus of the nations and peoples. There is her prestige, miraculous by origin, nurtured by hope, heightened by love, rendered steadfast by antiquity. There is the succession of bishops, beginning with the See of the Apostle Peter to whom the risen Lord committed the shepherding of His sheep, and continuing down to our present episcopate. Finally, there is the very name, Catholic, which in spite of the presence of so many heretical groups, she alone has achieved—and not without cause. Although all heretics want to be called Catholics, yet when a stranger asks one of them where the Catholic Church gathers, he does not dare to point to his own basilica or dwelling.[43]

We believe likewise in the holy Church—the Catholic Church, of course. It is true that heretics and schismatics call their congregations churches. But heretics, on the one hand, do violence to faith itself because they have false notions concerning God,

[49]

and schismatics, on the other hand, break away from the loving brotherhood by their unjustified secession, even though they believe the same things we do. In consequence, neither heretics belong to the Catholic Church, because she loves God, nor schismatics, because she loves the neighbor.[44]

According to this faith the Catholic tries to live and act. He cannot do otherwise; here he stands; God help him. Amen.

The Catholic takes seriously the prayer of Christ "that all may be one." But he desires thereby the ever greater union of Catholics among themselves and the introduction of the "other sheep," Christ's by uncovenanted mercies, into the one fold, so that there will be but one fold and one shepherd. By Catholic faith every Catholic is intensely ecumenist.

However, when ecumenism is understood as the current phenomenon best observed in the World Council of Churches, then Catholic ambivalence begins to manifest itself. His own generic ecumenism logically draws the Catholic's attention to the reunion movement surging so mightily outside of his own Church. It gives him hope that his own ecumenical desires may be at least in part fulfilled. He need not see the World Council as something strange and disturbing; for the Instruction of the Holy Office did not hesitate to call it the fruit of the inspiration of grace. In consequence, the Catholic's love, good wishes, and prayers move toward the World Council. But here the ambivalence goes to work. He does not want the World Council to continue in definitive existence. He wants it to bring all of its churches into the Catholic Church. He considers the Council good and grace-inspired insofar as it will bring the "other sheep" into the fold of the one Shepherd, visibly represented by His one vicar. He does not at all consider it good if it will only serve to stabilize the alienation of the "other sheep."

This attitude is not ambivalent, given the Catholic's inevitable point of departure, but it seems highly ambivalent to one whose starting point is utterly different. Let us see the other point of view.

Ever since the split between Byzantium and Rome, efforts have been made to heal the breach. Three councils were held to bring the two churches together. As we know, there was no great degree of success in the endeavors, but all saw that reunion was a highly desirable thing. After the Western split of Christendom in the sixteenth century, plans for reunion were not lacking. Calvin himself looked for the union of the evangelical churches, but he could not persuade the Lutherans to accept his followers in communion, and the free-spirit evangelicals, misleadingly labeled Anabaptists, were not too keen for an over-all union. Leibniz later certainly dreamed of and worked for reunion.

Bishop Brent's pain and dismay at the sight of Christian division in our time was more dynamic than in others, but as events clearly showed, he was not alone in longing for union. The evils of division, the irrationality of it, the scandals resulting are all visible and saddening. Unity is the wish of Christ; unity is the demand of reason; unity is the goal of love.

Christians of the Reform tradition by and large do not claim that their churches are the Church of Christ. Calvin and Luther localized the congregations, leaving the question of the Church somewhat vague. Calvin's famous dictum that you cannot point to the Church with your finger indicates that the Church and the congregation must not be identified. You could belong to a congregation which was not Calvinist and yet belong to the Church, just as you could belong to a Calvinistic congregation without belonging to the Church. Calvin was willing to have intercommunion with Lutherans, even though Luther himself had rebuffed such advances. But in principle Luther could have united with the Swiss churches. That is why he could enter into conversation with them for this purpose. On the other hand, neither Lutherans nor Calvinists, and much less the "free spirits," could in principle unite with the Catholic Church. This was clear to all concerned in the problem. Ecclesiology was not a reflex discipline in those days—and it is only coming of age in our time. But there were ecclesiologies at work in all of the different groups then in existence. An implicit and unexpressed ecclesiology is not the absence of ecclesiology. It is a very dangerous theology, because it is assumed, half-unconscious, and thus never subject to analysis and criticism. The idea that Christian doctrine can prescind from ecclesiology is an idle fantasy. It is always present, because *ekklesia* is a key doctrine of the New Testament, which is recognized by all as an authentic and normative description of Christian faith.

Dr. Visser't Hooft complains because Catholics always see an ecclesiology in the World Council. He insists that it has none, though he admits that ecclesiological assumptions are in operation. I submit with all candor and humility that this is not an adequate analysis of the phenomenon. The Council is a fellowship of *churches* by definition. Its hope is to "manifest" the *una sancta* ever more genuinely. You cannot say *una sancta* meaningfully unless you understand the noun that necessarily goes with it, and that noun is *ecclesia*. How, then, can one adequately say that the World Council has no ecclesiology? Rather one should say, how can it not have one? Just because it is assumed and unformulated hardly makes it less dynamic or less operative.

Of course, Dr. Visser't Hooft is pointing to something easily verifiable and altogether true, namely, that given the many ecclesiologies of the member churches, the Council itself makes none of them its own. Moreover, it deliberately and consciously avoids the formulation and imposition of an ecclesiology. This is not a lack of courage nor a failure to see the high import of ecclesiology, but only the charitable urge to offend no one in order to keep all together in love and harmony. Let love operate, and ecclesiology will take care of itself. The Spirit alone can unite Christians, and the Spirit operates in and through love, which He infuses into the hearts of men.

There is much in this presentation of the facts which is true. As a call to collaboration it is highly moving. It stirs the best instincts embedded in Christian faith. The Catholic feels it. Even the "outsiders" experience the "insider" pull. But Christian faith demands that we examine the pull before we allow ourselves to be drawn by it.

In the fourth chapter of the First Epistle of John, where the primacy of love is inculcated, we also find a precautionary introduction:

Beloved, do not believe every spirit, but test the spirits to see whether they are of God; for many false prophets have gone out into the world. . . . Little children, you are of God, and have overcome them; for he who is in you is greater than he who is in the world. They are of the world, therefore what they say is of the world, and the world listens to them. We are of God. Whoever knows God listens to us, and he who is not of God does not listen to us. By this we know the spirit of truth and the spirit of error.[45]

There is here an affirmation of the relevancy of the test of truth. Love is not to be identified with every upsurge of kindly feeling. The love Christians esteem so highly is the fruit of the Spirit who is the spirit of truth. If my feeling does not derive from this source, it is not the love of the gospel. True love is love in truth. Any other kind is not generative of the high goods enumerated in the thirteenth chapter of 1 Corinthians. In fact, it is quite capable of tragic destruction, as the Greek dramatists well showed.

Consequently, we must make some distinctions concerning the fruitfulness of the loving fellowship of all who claim the Christian name. If it is true love which kneads together the fellowship, it will begin in truth and enrich the vision of truth. If it be not love in truth, it will only obscure and mutilate truth. Lust is love. The will to possess is love. Calculated self-interest is a kind of love. Yet from these imperfect forms of love we need expect no lasting good. Not every kind of love is healthy; not every kind of love is creative. In a word, we must keep away from love rooted in delusion.

These are general ideas. They are not criticisms of the World Council. They only serve as a priori grounds for the criticism of a justification of the work and being of the Council by claiming it to be an exercise of love. In the light of our observations, such a justification cannot be ultimate; for it must ultimately show that the love at work in the Council is love in truth.

At this point the ambivalence is no longer on the Catholic side. It shows up crystal clear on the side of the non-Catholic ecumenists. I get the feeling that they are impatient of the question of truth and grow somewhat irritable when the question is raised. Of course we know they love the truth sincerely. Of course they want nothing but the truth. Of course they are searching for it and believe that man can find it. Theirs is not the stand of the sceptic or of the philosophic relativist. But truth is the word of God and "the word of God is living and active, sharper than the two-edged sword, piercing to the division of soul and spirit."[46] Whatever those words may mean, undoubtedly truth is divisive, but the Council wishes above all to be unitive. In consequence, it is unsure in its search for truth, torn by the hope that it will gradually be seen by all united, and by the fear that any heavy emphasis on it will break up the union.

One can easily object to all these reflections that they show beautifully the "outsider" mentality. If you shared the thrilling experience of harmonious collaboration and discussion, the exhilaration of common prayer, the transparent sincerity of intention in so many devout men and women, you would see at once that all your abstract difficulties are irrelevant. Because you have not felt all this, you can spin out your ivory-tower abstractions.

Is this answer really telling, or is it only avoiding the basic issue? Fortunately for the good of the Council itself, not all is sweetness and light at its meetings. There are deep conflicts which, because they are deep, are not always apparent on the surface. But they do manifest themselves at times in spite of the courtesy which is the soul of Council discussions. Sincerity, piety, devotion, and humble candor attract me to a man, but they are not proofs for the validity of the visions held by him, nor will they logically draw me to his beliefs any more than they will draw him to mine. When we do not agree, I am saddened, because I have learned to love my new friend, but I see that our oneness is going to be severely limited. If our disagreement is religious, our religious union will be thin. We shall be one in spite of it—but not in religious unity. And is not the World Council supposed to be a religious unity?

Human love, of course, can make me accept my friend's ideas. The long history of religious experience shows that, for love of man or maid, many a human being has left his or her previous religious faith. If the first faith was erroneous, its loss need not be regretted. If it was the truth, the man has rejected the revealing God—a fearful thing. Human love can produce either of the two changes.

Ah, but not love in the Spirit! Granted, but here again we must discern the spirits. It is moving to see so many workers of the Council give witness to the love they have encountered in their ecumenical work across denominational lines, and it is impressive to feel their conviction that the Spirit was at work. But their subjective estimate of what was going on carries no objective guaranty that they have judged the matter adequately. That the Spirit brought the ecumenists together was stated by the Instruction of the Holy Office. That the Spirit alone directs and guides the Council would be more than even ecumenists dare affirm.

In our time there is a reluctance to appeal to truth as normative for the affairs of men. This does not mean that our age as a whole is indifferent to truth or sceptical of man's capacity for achieving it. However, there is a widespread conviction that certain goods can be attained by

[56]

bracketing the question of truth, at least in the initial endeavors. This mind seems to be shared by the champions of the Council.

When we deal with the problem of church unity, this methodological principle implicitly asserts that unity of doctrine is not necessary, at least in the beginning. Here we have an ecclesiology. If Descartes gave us the methodic doubt to get out of doubt, this ecclesiology could be described as methodic indifferentism in order to overcome indifferentism. It is difficult to see how Catholics are wrong when they find that indifferentism is the great danger of present non-Catholic ecumenism.

Moreover, even methodic indifferentism is impossible for a Catholic. As he sees it, Christianity always demanded orthodox doctrine as the first requisite of union. It is not altogether objective to point to the infant Church as if it allowed any type of doctrine. If the Pauline epistles because of their obscurity appear to give us a picture of doctrinal diversity among the first Christians, the Johannine tradition clearly denies that such a situation is possible. Judaizers and gnostics are certainly excluded from the *ekklesia* according to Johannine texts. Even Paul makes it clear that the doctrine he taught must be preserved. The resurrection of Christ, for example, simply cannot be denied. That there would be a wider variety of opinion in the early days is to be expected. It would take time for doctrinal uniformity to harden, but the principle of doctrinal uniformity was stressed from the beginning. It seems clear enough that the one faith demanded by Paul is not merely the identical Christ-surrender of all Christians but also the acceptance of the one doctrine.

It is here that we find an innocent blindness in so many

non-Catholic ecumenists. They speak of the "rebuffs" of Rome, and this only means that Rome has consistently refused to take part in the non-Catholic ecumenical efforts. Those who speak of the "rebuffs" usually add with candor that there was no personal rejection, that every courtesy and good will was manifested to the persons who made overtures to the Catholics for collaboration.

The historical fact is that every living non-Catholic Christian community broke away from the Catholic Church. Some did it immediately; others split away from the churches which had previously done so. The Nestorians and Monophysites broke with the ecumenical Church, but there was no doubt where the ecumenical Church was. Constantinople represented the ecumene for the East and Rome represented it for the West. When Michael Caerularius in the eleventh century occasioned the definitive separation of Constantinople and Rome, there was no doubt in the mind of either East or West that the ecumenical Church was identified either with the Byzantine or with the Roman communion. For the Orient, Rome and the West were in heresy and therefore out of the Church; and for Rome, the "Greeks" were in schism and therefore out of the Church. The two sections were in perfect agreement that one or the other was the ecumenical church—not that both were. The Eastern Orthodox and the Catholics to this day maintain the same positions.

Today the Byzantine Orientals are in the Council. Whether they can consistently be there is a question for them to solve, but they are well aware of that question. Some of their delegates at Council meetings are uncomfortable and wonder if they should be there at all. Others believe that it is an admirable and charitable medium for giving witness to the truth which is fully contained exclusively in the Eastern Byzantine communities and which all others must accept in order to be truly in the Church of Christ. None has the intention of forming or entering a union which will be anything else than the Eastern Church as it is structured today. If Anglicans or others want intercommunion with the Byzantines, they must *first* as churches accept the dogmas of Byzantine belief. The question of valid succession and sacraments can be discussed only after that initial unity in *belief* is established.

When Orientals and Catholics hold dialogue, this point is so clear to both that there is never any ambiguity. Both know that what is called for by the other party in the dialogue is agreement on doctrine. One side is wrong and the other is right, and the side in the wrong must accept the right side before any reunion is possible. There never is the supposition that neither side is right and both are wrong, that neither is the Church but both are only defective phases of it. Neither do the Byzantines within the Council today believe that any church within the fellowship has any title, even partial, to the name of the Church of Christ except their own church. According to their theory, this is the Church into which the others must enter, and it visibly exists today without waiting for some future time for its manifestation.

Sometimes one doubts if non-Catholic ecumenists really know what they do when they invite the Catholic Church to enter into a fellowship on the basis that they are somehow the Church of Christ. (Many non-Catholics do not want her invited!) Logically enough, Protestants insist on the validity of the action and fundamental positions of the Reformers in the sixteenth century. It is hard to see how they could be Protestants if they denied such validity. However, in affirming the position of the Reformers they must accept the consequences which the Reformers were courageous enough (as a Protestant would judge) or rash enough (as the Catholic thinks) to accept. The consequence was that they declared the Catholic Church to be an apostate church, and they in turn were considered heretical by the Catholic Church. The only logical thing for the Protestants is to ask the Catholic Church to become converted to Protestantism; for how can they ask an apostate church to enter into union with the Church of Christ without conversion? If the Catholics come to their union, some slight degree of conversion is already achieved. This is tantamount to suicide for the Catholic Church, and an invitation to suicide may be courteous in form but it is hardly gracious in substance.

This kind of reflection will strike non-Catholic ecumenists as being a mere exercise in logical subtleties. No one is asking the Catholic Church to change her views. But let us all come together and air our views. No more is being asked.

But there are assumptions at work in this seemingly reasonable stand. Non-Catholics know quite well what Catholics believe. There is no secret about it, because it is candidly and forthrightly stated over and over again. Bishop Stephen Charles Neill, a leading figure of the World Council, in a context somewhat different from ours, says:

We are at a great advantage in dealing with our Roman Catholic friends, because we know exactly where we are with them, and, if we are deluded, it is our own fault. . . . But I know exactly where I am with a Roman Catholic friend, and I do not regard him as uncharitable for holding a view to which, however untenable I may myself regard it as being, he is pledged as long as he remains a member of that Church.[47]

It seems to me that so many Protestants, with the best of good will, always hope that the Catholic Church has finally "come to her senses" and, if face can be saved, will retreat from her exclusivist position. This seems to them all that a reasonable man could do and they are handsomely prepared to recognize reasonableness in Catholics. They are too intelligent and too human to brand all Catholics as either fools or knaves. After all, Protestantism has relinquished so much of its characteristic stands and is willing to relinquish more. The Catholics certainly cannot be different. The tacit assumption is that all the churches have erred grievously, even in matters of substance. The tacit assumption is that the Church of Christ is an ideal which has never been actual in history, nor ever will be, though we can do much to approximate the ideal more closely. The tacit assumption is that all Christians belong to this Church of Christ, in spite of their defects, errors, and sins.

This is an ecclesiology. It is not a very satisfactory one, because it abounds in ambiguities of the most trying kind. Yet this ecclesiology must be accepted, at least for the sake of discussion, in order to enter the World Council. To say, therefore, that the Council has no ecclesiology is to refuse to reflect on the reality before us.

This ecclesiology, unrecognized though it be, cannot be accepted by a Catholic, not even as the starting point of discussion. The instructed Catholic, who knows that he can lose his grace of faith, can speculate on what would be his position in such an hypothetical event. The vast majority thinks that the only rational alternative to Catholicism is

[61]

the complete rejection of Christianity. The average Catholic considers non-Catholic forms of Christianity either as rationally inconsistent or as not coherent with the facts of life and history. For him anything less than Catholicism is a *reductio ad absurdum* of Christianity, and the Council is, to say the least, prepared to accept something less than Catholicism.

I do not say these things to irritate non-Catholics. I pass over the question whether the Catholic conception is justified. I wish only to state that it is here as a palpable fact. The Catholic accepts as a fact that non-Catholics do not share his views, though it puzzles him. Is it too much to ask the non-Catholic to recognize the Catholic fact, puzzling though it may be?

It is at this point that the Catholic's ambivalence again shows up. He has no ill will for the World Council and its kindred associations. On the contrary, he gives them his best wishes. He cannot help but be critical, with the criticism of an "outsider." His criticisms are not the fruit of hostility but the result of sober reflection on the meaning of non-Catholic ecumenism when compared with the Catholic's own fundamental ecclesiology, implicit or explicit, reflex or spontaneous.

Do non-Catholic ecumenists see this? They always seem to see the sinister shadow of Roman despotism in the Catholic aloofness to the World Council. Yet there has been no such despotism. The Roman norms, according so perfectly with Catholic doctrine, are not arbitrary or wilful. It is hard to see what else the Roman authorities could have done, and what they have done was always couched with great respect and deference to the good will of the non-Catholics involved. But non-Catholics should see that, given the structure and the scope of the World Council as we now have it, Catholic formal and active participation is out of the question. Should the Council change its scope and assumptions, a new situation would arise, but it is fruitless to determine what Catholics would then do, unless a concrete rather than an abstract hypothesis be considered. To propose or answer hypothetical questions seems singularly futile at the moment.

The good will which the Catholic feels for non-Catholic ecumenism leads him to effective action. One thing he can do and he is doing it. He can pray. Father Paul's Church Unity Octave is a widespread Catholic prayer. Msgr. Couturier's modification of it is equally widespread. Non-Catholics seem to prefer the Couturier formula, but let them remember that Father Paul and Couturier both understood Church unity as the union of all Christians *within* the Catholic Church, not outside of it. The Graymoor prayers candidly state what Couturier had in mind without stating it, namely, the return of non-Catholic Christians to the unity of the Church visibly centered in the Bishop of Rome. If Msgr. Couturier's prayer wanted anything else, it would hardly have been the sincere prayer of a Catholic, and he was very Catholic indeed. Non-Catholics must not think that the vaguer formula is a sign of receding from this central point. Msgr. Couturier's modification was justified by him on practical rather than dogmatic grounds. He felt that the immediate raising of the doctrine of papal primacy would repel non-Catholics, but he knew that they would have to face it ultimately. There is Catholic division on the wisdom of Couturier's approach. Some think that the fundamental question should be raised at once; others think it should be delayed until a more favorable climate for it is produced. This is the only difference to be found in divergent Catholic ecumenical activities, a difference of method but not a difference of goal. Any Catholic ecumenist believes that the Church of Christ is Roman and papal. When he begins to doubt that, he is not of us.

Nor is the Catholic ecumenist content with prayer alone. He is anxious to talk to non-Catholics. He is anxious to give information to non-Catholic ecumenists, and the World Council never has had difficulty in finding competent Catholics to give it any information it wanted. The Catholic Church is not a secret society, and the liturgical *disciplina arcani* disappeared almost fifteen hundred years ago. Roman directives have given norms for such indirect collaboration, and the norms are intended to eliminate irresponsible statements which could mislead non-Catholics or foster false hopes in them. There is a constant danger of false irenicism, as *Humani generis* pointed out. Msgr. Ronald Knox translated the word brilliantly when he rendered it as a "policy of appeasement."[48] To a generation still mindful of the "peace in our time" slogan with its disastrous Munich compromise, appeasement is not a golden word. As long as the Catholic is Catholic and the Protestant is Protestant, there is only one way to union—the conversion of one to the views of the other. If that should happen, either Catholicism or Protestantism would disappear. There can never be a Catholic-Protestant Church, or even a Catholic-Protestant fellowship of churches. This is the basic fact. It does no good to anyone to hope that this fact will somehow sublimate into something thinner.

Because the Catholic recognizes this fact clearly and unambiguously, his ecumenical strivings are more consistent.

He knows what is called for, and he moves toward the goal of the conversion of the non-Catholic.

Yet this very clarity of objectives produces for the Catholic serious problems in the practical order. The old days, when Catholics in large numbers believed that all Protestants were wilful heretics with contumacity in their hearts, are gone. There are relatively few countries where Protestants are not highly visible, and so many Catholics are closely tied with the bonds of friendship or links of kinship with Protestants. The virtues of the Protestant are everywhere to see and his good will is quite tangible. The sincerity of his faith is unquestioned. Yet that faith must oppose him to Catholicism. If the Reform was right in substance, then Catholicism is in substance wrong. Protestants today are quite willing to see that much in the Reform was needless and even detrimental. Hence we have the Protestant liturgical movement, the recognition of the inevitability of tradition as a compart to Scripture, the legitimacy and even necessity of episcopacy, the return to auricular confession, the unity and visibility of the Church, and many other facets which tended to disappear in the Reform revolution. But the rejection of the guiding, ruling, sanctifying, teaching Church through authoritative organs within its visible structure is as strong today as ever.

On the Catholic side there is also the awareness that the Reform was not lacking in prophetic inspiration, even though it lacked the prophetic charism. There was much which the Reformers criticized which the Catholic admits was worthy of adverse judgment. Under the divinely permitted blows of the scourge of secession, he forced himself to correct abuses. However, the Catholic still believes and will always believe that the nuclear character of the Reform movement was irreconcilable with the gospel and a contradiction of the faith once delivered to the saints. The dynamism of the Reform tended to rend the seamless robe of Christ, and certainly tore a valuable piece of it off.

How, in spite of this radical divergence, can the Catholic meet the Protestant amicably and fruitfully in the ecumenical encounter? This is the Catholic's practical problem. The Protestant's willingness to revise his evaluation of the Reform certainly is a help. But the Protestant's insistence that the Catholic Church was just as wrong as the Reformers is no help at all. The Catholic must say to the Protestant that the Church was substantially right, and therefore any endeavor toward reunion will be a return to her unreconstructed, unreformed unity.

For Protestants this is a hard saying, and who can listen to it? It seems obvious enough that we cannot begin conversations at that crucial point. Instead, we must speak about the notion of revelation and the notion of the Church. These larger themes are not immediately irritating, although it will not be long before they become so. We all know how important it is to understand the neighbor. Words are not univocal, even when pronounced with utter sincerity. They shade off into unstressed negations and affirmations. The essay at understanding is itself a salutary experience, usually producing a heightened esteem for the other man. Esteem brings with it some degree of love.

It would seem clear enough, in the light of the experience of centuries, that polemic and controversy will not be an effective encounter. Name-calling is a childish device, pardonable in children perhaps, but certainly regrettable in adults. It is consoling that in this our time the tendency to name-calling is well under control in all. Forthrightness in the expression of views and positions is not name-calling. We need it. We must know where we stand, and slurring or double-talk will not advance the investigation. Yet some words are heavily charged with emotion, because they were rubbed by history. Nor can they be avoided. But, as far as possible, they must be deprived of their emotional charge and considered as symbols of thought, emotionally neutral. This is no easy thing, but it is not altogether impossible. A word like "Luther" or "pope" does not today exercise the sensitivities of other times. The word "Jesuit" has lost most of its sinister connotation. A functional vocabulary is undoubtedly at hand.

Certainly patience will be required. Both Catholic and non-Catholic ecumenists know that man cannot bring about the union of all who profess the Christian name. That is God's work, and under His grace the work will proceed. It is not for us to tell the Lord what He has to do, but rather accept gladly His plans and purposes. This necessity for patience is no obstacle to the work; for it will be the best antidote against the frustration arising out of the seeming failure of any given moment. We are in God's hands, and it is His will which we seek and not our own. We see the necessity of working for reunion, because such is His will, and that is reason enough for doing it. Success is not the proper goal of human effort.

How and where shall we meet? There is no simple answer to that question. Certainly there is much being written in our day, and we are reading each other's message. Informal meetings are surely easiest for all concerned. There is something highly attractive in the work of the group patronized by the Archbishop of Paderborn. Excellently prepared men both in the Catholic and Lutheran camps meet in friendship and obvious good will. A Catholic bishop gives responsibility and security to the contributions of the Catholics. There is little danger of unhappy formulas and exaggerations engendered by romantic enthusiasm uncontrolled by sober realism.

The danger which must be avoided is the mere exuberance of the heart. That organ may well have its reasons which reason does not know, but without the resonance of the heart with reason informed by knowledge, action can degenerate into sheer sound and fury, signifying nothing.

The immediate objective of such meetings should be clarification of positions and ultimate differences. This clarification will demand the transposition of themes from one terminology and one standpoint into the language and concern of the other. This is no easy task, because the dynamism of much of any man's thought is found in unrecognized assumptions. To get these assumptions out into the open requires cool analysis and kindly objectivity.

A lesser task will be the recognition of agreement in certain slogans and formulas which appear contradictory but are not. There are many things Catholics and non-Catholics hold in common, even though they may express themselves differently. To anyone engaged in ecumenical study it soon becomes clear that some of the controversial issues of the past were, in the light of today, needlessly raised. As an example we might point to the question of faith. That word has a different meaning for Catholic and Protestant, but strangely enough the Protestant does not really deny what the Catholic holds under the label, nor does the Catholic deny the characteristic value of Protestant faith which the Catholic calls hope and charity. They are not talking about the same thing when they use the word "faith." But this is being ever more abundantly recognized by current scholars. The fruitful scriptural studies made today by Catholics and non-Catholics, where a great degree of agreement is achieved, has brought the scholars of the two camps closer together, because they rely in part on each other's work.

One conclusion which seems to follow from these reflections is that the mission of ecumenist encounter falls primarily on the Catholic theologian. He is in the best position to understand his side and the other. Once more it must be stressed that understanding is the *conditio sine qua non* for fertile conversation either in writing or in the spoken word.

For Catholic theologians this truth implies an obligation. Our theology has consistency and stability because of long existence. Catholic theologians consciously and lovingly keep within the method rooted in the work of St. Thomas. This has given our theology its cohesive vitality, and it would be silly and wrong to change this. However, for ecumenical work more must be done. The task does not mean that we must scrap our own precious heritage, but we must in addition build something parallel to it. We must follow the example of Thomas in more than his structural method. With sympathetic insight he went into the thought of those who were outside of the Catholic theological tradition. He immersed himself in the works of men like Aristotle, Ibn Sina, and Ibn Rushd, so that he became a perennial authority on their thought. They did not make him less a Catholic theologian but rather more so. He was not alienated from his own family because he thoroughly studied the mind of those beyond it.

There must today be more Catholic study of non-Catholic positions. This was the explicit counsel of *Humani generis,* silencing in advance any objections which might have been raised by theological xenophobes.[49] If the Pope's counsel was good for Catholic thinkers everywhere in the world, it was perhaps most timely for American theologians, who by and large have not been too aware of their obligation, even though most pressing in our cultural climate, of which pluralism is the specific note.

Again we note a propitious moment for study of this kind. In the past, great theologians like St. Robert Bellarmine, Francisco Suárez, and Johann Adam Möhler dug deeply into Protestant theology. Their work was good and was so recognized by all. Unfortunately, so many of their epigoni did not live up to the level of their masters. With a spirit of unconcealed hostility the later men reduced the serene work of their predecessors to a ludicrous caricature of the original positions, and for many years this caricature was palmed off to innocent and ignorant tyros as the whole truth. Is it too fantastic to think that, for many a Catholic student of theology, *pecca fortiter sed fortius fide*[50] is the formula which genuinely, adequately, and loyally expresses the complete thought of Luther? Today, fortunately, we find a widespread discomfort with this kind of presentation.

One cannot begin a work of study with the antecedent decision to refute the thought of the author to be studied. With such a spirit animating the whole investigation, nothing valuable will come of it. One reads in order to learn. A Catholic does not go to non-Catholic sources in order to learn the revelation of Christ, because by Catholic faith he finds the revelation in the teaching of the magisterium, whose instruments are the Scriptures enveloped and illuminated by the different forms of tradition. However, he can learn, first of all, what the other man said. In his essay at learning he might well take into account the wise advice of Ignatius of Loyola in his introduction to the *Exercises:*

. . . the presumption is that a good Christian should be more prone to save the proposition of the neighbor than to condemn it. If, indeed, he cannot save it, let him inquire how the neighbor understands it. If this understanding of it be bad, let the Christian correct the neighbor with love. Should this be insufficient, let him take all suitable measures to make the proposition acceptable by giving it a good meaning.[51]

This insight of a saint of the Church will serve as a sound norm for the Church's theologians.

One more truth the Catholic theologian must bear in mind. The ecumenist apostolate is not the formal task of theology. It is a by-product. The theologian by definition does theology, and in doing it performs his proper function in the Church. He is a contemplative primarily, though from the overflow of his contemplation the neighbor's thirst for light and knowledge can be slaked or sated. The non-contemplative apostolate striving for the unity of all Christians is a specifically different activity of the Church. In consequence, the theologian will do this work of the Church under the direction of the members of the Mystical Body structured and empowered for the work of guidance. These directors, the episcopal regimen, have a charism for their function. The theologian does not immediately share in that charism, though he has the charism for theological meditation and exposition. The ecumenist theologian, in consequence, works with and for the regimen. He is not independent of it. Regiminal norms, therefore, will be the framework of his ecumenical apostolate.

This reflection may help to allay impatience. The theologian, rightly or wrongly, may see that such and such a technique or tactic is the rational demand of some determined moment. The regimen, on the other hand, may not see it that way. Now human vision is limited and the human evaluation of an historical moment is fallible. However, the charism in the rectors leads them by a force which is more than human, and by our faith we know that this force is the Holy Spirit Himself. God's ways are not our ways, and God's judgments take into account all the factors involved in reality, factors invisible to the human spectator. Under God's guidance the regimen works, and even its human deficiencies help to bring about the divine good planned for us all.

If, then, the theologian feels himself at times hampered or slowed down, he by his knowledge, more than others, should see that no divinely intended good is being blocked. In God's will is our peace. Besides, the charismatic influence in the rectors securely grounds the presumption of the adequacy of their vision and leadership. Moreover, even the best of theologians is always a very fallible man whose intellect is darkened and whose will is to some degree perverted by reason of the original fall.

★ Notes ★

[1] The use of the word "ecumenical" has an interesting history. In *A History of the Ecumenical Movement,* ed. Ruth Rouse and Stephen Charles Neill (Philadelphia: Westminster Press, 1954) p. 735, W. A. Visser't Hooft outlines the use of the word as follows: "In the course of history we can distinguish seven meanings of the word 'ecumenical': (a) pertaining to or representing the whole (inhabited) earth; (b) pertaining to or representing the whole of the (Roman) Empire; (c) pertaining to or representing the whole of the Church; (d) that which has universal ecclesiastical validity; (e) pertaining to the world-wide missionary outreach of the Church; (f) pertaining to the relations between and unity of two or more Churches (or of Christians of various confessions); (g) that quality or attitude which expresses the consciousness of and desire for Christian unity." Visser't Hooft has also published a longer study on the subject, *The Meaning of Ecumenical* (London: S.C.M. Press, 1953).

In profane Greek as well as in the New Testament, "ecumenical" has the meanings labeled (a) and (b). In the post-Nicene patristic Church and after, the word signifies the content of (c) and (d). In the last century among Protestants the word conveyed the meaning of (e). Since the birth of the Faith and Order, and Life and Work movements the word is used in the sense of (f) and (g). Today (g) defines the word in its current usage.

Prof. Carl F. H. Henry, editor of the conservative evangelical journal, *Christianity Today* (Washington), discusses the word in a mimeographed conference on Christian unity, *The Unity Christ Sustains.* His point of view is restrictedly scriptural, and in the light of the New Testament he says: "In none of the fifteen New Testament occurrences is the term *oikoumene* equated with the church, but rather with the world to which the church witnesses" (p. 4). Dr. Visser't Hooft would not deny this, but he rejects any notion implying that in the New Testament "ecumenical" had a hostile meaning for the Christians.

[2] The spelling of "ecumenism" is fluid. In the Roman documents, for its modern use, the word ecumenical is written as *oecumenicum* and put in in-

verted commas; the Germans and French use "oe" rather than a plain "e"; in English both spellings are found, but the simple "e" is far more common. The derivatives "ecumenist" and "ecumenism" also appear as "ecumenicist" and "ecumenicism." In my article in *Thought* 30 (1955) 5–17, "Ecumenicism and the Catholic," I used the latter spelling, but it seems that "ecumenist" and "ecumenism" are more widely used.

[3] *The First Assembly of the World Council of Churches* (Official report), ed. W. A. Visser't Hooft (New York: Harper, 1949) p. 267.

[4] The constitution as adopted at Amsterdam can be found in the Official Report (cf. note 3) pp. 196 ff. The rules appear in the same volume, pp. 202 ff. In this study we shall use the amended texts as they appear in *The Evanston Report. The Second Assembly of the World Council of Churches, 1954*, ed. W. A. Visser't Hooft (New York: Harper, 1955). Constitution: pp. 337 ff. Rules: pp. 342 ff.

[5] *Britannica Book of the Year, 1956* (Chicago: Encyclopedia Britannica, Inc., 1956) p. 636.

[6] *The First Assembly of the World Council of Churches*, p. 231.

[7] *The Evanston Report*, pp. 300–301.

[8] The figures for the different denominations are taken from *Yearbook of American Churches for 1958* (New York: National Council of Churches of Christ in the U.S.A., 1957) pp. 13 ff. The *Yearbook* also gives the personnel of the World Council and its committees; cf. pp. 118–19.

[9] For names of committees and their secretaries, cf. note 8.

[10] The constitution of the Faith and Order Commission is given in *The Third World Conference on Faith and Order*, ed. Oliver S. Tomkins (London: S.C.M. Press, 1953) pp. 359 ff.

[10a] Concerning this conference, cf. Gustave Weigel, S.J., "Faith and Order at Oberlin," *America* 98, n. 3 (October 19, 1957) 67–71.

[11] *A History of the Ecumenical Movement, 1517–1948*, ed. Ruth Rouse and Stephen Charles Neill (Philadelphia: Westminster Press, 1954). This work contains a good bibliography on ecumenism. An excellent bibliography on reunion work and thought can also be found in Henry R. T. Brandreth, *Unity and Reunion. A Bibliography* (London: Adam & Charles Black, 1945).

[12] Walter Marshall Horton, *Christian Theology—An Ecumenical Approach* (New York: Harper, 1955).

[13] W. A. Visser't Hooft, "Notes on Roman Catholic Writings concerning Ecumenism," *Ecumenical Review* 8 (1956) 191–97.

[14] David Gannon, S.A., *Father Paul of Graymoor* (New York: Macmillan, 1951).

[15] Lillian Stevenson, *Max Josef Metzger, Priest and Martyr* (New York: Macmillan, 1952).

[16] *Acta apostolicae sedis* 19 (1927) 278. Henceforth we shall refer to the *Acta* by the usual abbreviation, *AAS*.

[17] *AAS* 11 (1919) 309.

[18] Henry Smith Leiper, *Relations between the Ecumenical Movement and*

the Vatican in the Twentieth Century. Mimeographed memorandum (New York: World Council of Churches, n.d.) p. 3.

19 *AAS* 20 (1928) 5–16. English translation: *Catholic Mind* 26 (1928) 61–72.

20 *AAS* 40 (1948) 257.

21 Official Report, pp. 236 ff.; cf. Rule II, 2, pp. 203–4; *The Evanston Report,* p. 344.

22 *AAS* 42 (1950) 142–47. English translation: *Instruction on the Ecumenical Movement* (Graymoor, Garrison, N.Y.: National Office of the Chair of Unity Octave, n.d.). To the translation is added a commentary by William Conway, originally appearing in *Irish Ecclesiastical Record* 73 (1950) 360–65.

23 *History,* Rouse and Neill, pp. 685–86; cf. p. 588 for a similar collaboration at the Oxford meeting of Life and Work.

24 *The Third World Conference,* p. 358.

25 *Who's Who, Wer ist's, Qui êtes-vous? (Lund, 1952):* Revised edition and list of delegates. *Faith and Order Commission Papers* 13 (1952) 67–68.

26 Cf. *The Universal Church in God's Design,* in the Amsterdam Assembly Series, *Man's Disorder and God's Design* (New York: Harper, 1949) pp. 169–76: "A Supplementary Note by a Roman Catholic Writer: Fr. Maurice Villain." Likewise in the report of the Theological Commission of the World Conference on Faith and Order, *Intercommunion,* ed. Donald Baillie and John Marsh (New York: Harper, 1952), Yves M.-J. Congar, O.P., contributed *"Amica contestatio,"* pp. 141–51.

27 W. A. Visser't Hooft, "Notes on Roman Catholic Writings," *Ecumenical Review* 8 (1956) 191.

28 Freiburg i. Br.: Herder, 1929. See also Pribilla's little brochure, *Die Una Sancta Bewegung* (Meitingen: Kyrios Verlag, 1948).

29 Translated by M. A. Bousfield (London: Geoffrey Bles, 1939). The French original was *Chrétiens désunis* (Paris: Editions du Cerf, 1937).

30 Paris, 1927.

31 A. Rademacher, *Die Wiedervereinigung christlicher Kirchen* (Bonn, 1937); *id., Der religiöse Sinn unserer Zeit und der ökumenische Gedanke* (Bonn, 1939); Karl Adam, *The One and Holy,* tr. Cecily Hastings (New York: Sheed and Ward, 1951). The German original of Adam's work was *Una Sancta in katholischer Sicht* (Düsseldorf: Patmos Verlag, 1948).

32 Charles Boyer, S.J., *One Shepherd,* tr. Angeline Bouchard (New York: Kenedy, 1952). The French original was *Unus pastor* (Toulouse: Apostolat de la Prière, 1950). Laros' work was published in Recklinghausen: Paulus Verlag, 1950.

33 Louvain: Ed. Warny, 1955.

34 Meitingen: Kyrios Verlag, 1955.

35 Washington: Catholic University Press, 1953.

36 New York: Harper, 1954. This work is Fr. Tavard's English revision of his French *A la rencontre du Protestantisme* (Paris: Le Centurion, 1954).

37 Cf. Msgr. Fenton's review of Tavard's book, *American Ecclesiastical Re-*

view 133 (1955) 352–53. See also Fenton's article, "Appraisal in Sacred Theology," *ibid.* 134 (1956) 23–36.

[38] "Sur la théologie du Conseil oecuménique," *Gregorianum* 35 (1954) 591–607. On p. 603, note 37 reads as follows: "On trouvera la doctrine catholique exposée avec sa documentation dans *Catholic Ecumenism,* par le P. Edward F. Hanahoe, S.A., Washington, 1953."

[39] "Qu'est, théologiquement à ses propres yeux le Conseil oecuménique des églises?," *Istina* 1 (1954) 389–407. Cf. likewise Hamer's "Mission de l'oecuménisme catholique," *Lumière et vie,* no. 19, pp. 65–82.

[40] A work not mentioned by Visser't Hooft but noteworthy at least for its sheer volume (710 pages) is the collection of studies presented at the Twelfth Spanish Theological Week, Sept. 17–22, 1952, *XII Semana Española de Teología. El Movimiento Ecumenista* (Madrid: C.S.I.C. Instituto "Francisco Suárez," 1953).

[41] The reference is to the article described in note 13.

[42] *De vera religione* 7, 12 (*PL* 34, 128).

[43] *Contra epistulam Manichaei* 4, 5 (*PL* 42, 175).

[44] *De fide et symbolo* 10, 21 (*PL* 40, 193).

[45] 1 Jn 4:1–6.

[46] Heb 4:12.

[47] *The Ministry of the Church,* ed. Bishop Stephen Neill (London and Edinburgh: Canterbury Press, 1947) p. 25.

[48] *Humani generis,* August 12, 1950; *AAS* 42 (1950) 564; tr. R. A. Knox, *Tablet* (London), Sept. 2, 1950, p. 187.

[49] "All this, evidently, concerns our own Catholic theologians and philosophers. They have a grave responsibility for defending truth, both divine and human, and for instilling it into men's minds; they must needs acquaint themselves with all these speculations, to a more or less extent erroneous; they must needs take them into account. Nay, it is their duty to have a thorough understanding of them. There is no curing a disease unless you have made a study of its symptoms. Moreover, there is some truth underlying even these wrongheaded ideas; yes, and they spur the mind on to study and to weigh certain truths, philosophical and theological, more carefully than we otherwise should." *AAS* 42 (1950) 563; tr. R. A. Knox, *Tablet* (London), Sept. 2, 1950, p. 187.

[50] In de Wette's edition of the Luther letters, Letter 332: *Briefe, Sendschreiben und Bedenken,* ed. Wilhelm de Wette. Part 2 (Berlin, 1826), Letter of August 1, 1521, to Melanchthon, p. 37.

[51] *Exercitia spiritualia sancti patris Ignatii de Loyola. Textus hispanus et versio litteralis Autographi hispani auctore A. R. P. Joanne Roothaan . . . ex editione quarta romana anni 1852* (Turin and Rome: Marietti, 1928) pp. 32, 33, n. [22].

⋆ Index ⋆

[77]